BURT FRANKLIN: RESEARCH & SOURCE WORKS SERIES
American Classics in History and Social Science 251

Judicial Interpretation of Political Theory

Judicial Interpretation of Political Theory

A Study in the Relation of the Courts to the American Party System

By

William Bennett Bizzell, D.C.L.

President of the College of Industrial Arts

BURT FRANKLIN REPRINTS
New York, N. Y.

Published by LENOX HILL Pub. & Dist. Co. (Burt Franklin)
235 East 44th St., New York, N.Y. 10017
Reprinted: 1974
Printed in the U.S.A.

Burt Franklin: Research and Source Works Series
American Classics in History and Social Science 251

Library of Congress Cataloging in Publication Data

Bizzell, William Bennett, 1876-1944.
  Judicial interpretation of political theory.

  Reprint of the 1914 ed. published by Putnam, New York.
    1. Judicial review—United States. 2. Political questions and judicial power
—United States. I. Title.
KF4575.B5 1974   342'.73'044   73-21602
ISBN 0-8337-4819-X

PREFACE

IN this age of the making of many books an explanation for publication is always in order. The contents of this volume consist in the main of a series of lectures delivered at the Illinois College of Law in 1910, and subsequently printed and used in the extension department of that institution. The chapters on "The Theory of Direct Legislation" and "The Theory of the Recall of Judicial Decisions" have been added to the original series especially for this volume, as these theories have developed since the original lectures were prepared. It is easy to see that by the use of copious quotations this volume could have been greatly extended, but an attempt has been made to present only the essential teachings of the authorities in order to make the trend of the argument clear. In the accomplishment of this task I fear that some important decisions have been omitted that should have been included.

The writer had no idea at the time the original lectures were prepared that the courts of the country were destined to come in for such a wide share of political attention as they have in so short a time. But such a study as this must convince any one that the increased opportunity of the courts to pass on questions of partisan and political views must eventually direct the attention of the public more and more to this unusual power of the courts, and that the courts will not be able to escape popular criticism. The wide attention that this question must attract in the immediate future is the excuse for the publication of this volume.

W. B. B.

COLLEGE OF INDUSTRIAL ARTS,
April 15, 1914.

CONTENTS

Judicial Interpretation of Political Theory

INTRODUCTION

WE are told by Professor Ellwood in a recent book[1] that "Highly dynamic societies control social activities by what is known as public opinion. Public opinion is not found to any extent in savage and barbarous societies, because social tradition takes its place. By public opinion we mean a more or less *rational collective judgment* formed by the action and re-action of many individual opinions upon one another." Under our system governmental policies crystallize out of public opinion, and the "collective judgment" resulting therefrom finds expression in our party system of politics. The social judgment which is the product of the collective opinion of a party has, in more recent times, found expression in a party platform. The aim of party activity has been in every case to give these social judgments the force of law, for this is

[1] *Sociology in its Psychological Aspects* (1912), p. 334.

the only way by which their real merits or demerits can be shown.

In the course of our political history the number of these social judgments has been numerous, the economic, political, and social changes of each decade tending to multiply them, and the parties themselves have created issues in order to give more distinct emphasis to certain beliefs deemed of paramount importance. But of the great number that have become of sufficient consequence to secure party recognition, few have been of fundamental and permanent significance. Some, however, have involved great principles of government and their relation to our organic law has been a matter of fundamental importance. Among these may be named the judicial theory of constitutional construction, the nature of the Federal Union, the policy of expansion (Imperialism v. Expansion), the theory of a national bank, the theory of legal tender, the protective tariff, internal improvements, and the income tax. About these great questions political debate has raged and learned and profound judicial opinions have been rendered by the most powerful judicial tribunal on the earth.

No student of our political history can fail to discern the important function the Supreme Court has performed in giving its stamp of approval to the social judgments of parties, or in pointing out the fallacies therein. And the uniformly high integrity of the members of the Court throughout its history, together with its dignity and learning, has been the safeguard against violence and factional conflict during several crises in our history. Webster's eulogy of the Court deserves wide dissemination:

" No conviction is deeper in my mind than that the maintenance of the judicial power is essential and indispensable to the very being of this Government. The Constitution, without it, would be no Constitution—the Government, no Government. I am deeply sensible, too, and, as I think, every man must be whose eyes have been opened to what has passed around him for the last twenty years, that the judicial power is the protecting power of the Government. Its position is upon the outer wall. From the very nature of things, and the frame of the Constitution, it forms the point at which our different systems of government meet in collision, when collision unhappily exists. By the absolute necessity of the case the members of the Supreme Court become judges of the extent of constitutional powers. They are, if I may so call them, the great arbitrators between contending sovereignties."[1]

Horace Binney had this function of the great Court in mind when he characterized it as "the great moral substitute for force in controversies between the people, the states, and the Union."

But we are not to infer that the members of the Supreme Court have always been able to free

[1] From a speech delivered in the House of Representatives, January 25, 1826.

themselves from party conviction. In fact, there
is ample evidence throughout our Federal decisions that members of our Supreme Court, while
not debasing their decisions with political doctrine,
at the same time found ways to give force and
effect to political theories advocated by them and
by their respective parties. Carson in his monu-
mental work on the history of the Supreme Court
discusses the influence of party convictions on
judicial decisions as follows:

"The theories of the Constitution entertained
by Marshall and Taney were those of their respective parties, and are irreconcilable. Without
imputing to either a desire to extend unnecessarily
or immoderately the doctrines of their schools,
it can be safely asserted that although partisan
politics should have no place upon the Bench, yet
it is impossible to expect men to divest themselves
of certain fundamental views in relation to the
nature of our Government simply because they
have ascended the Bench and thrown aside the
contentions of the political arena."[1]

The reason that personal convictions often
find expression in the decisions handed down from
the Bench is that the law is not an exact science
like mathematics. As Herbert Broom[2] has said:
"The law, while it concerns itself mainly with
principles, is not a fixed science. Its definitions
are not fixed and determinate like those of ge-
ometry, and are not therefore, and cannot in the

[1] Vol. ii., p. 380.   [2] *Philosophy of Law*, Preface, p. vi.

nature of things be, certainly and positively expressed. A judge never decides general principles. He decides a case." It is this characteristic of the law that makes room for the traditional beliefs and personal convictions of those who interpret it. The influence of these convictions may be easily illustrated from a few conspicuous examples.

John Marshall was appointed Chief Justice in 1801. He was a Virginian by birth, and had seen service in the Revolutionary War. He had served as a member of the Lower House in his native state, and had been a member of the Executive Council. When the question of the adoption of the Federal Constitution came up, he was one of the leaders in urging its adoption by the people. He and Madison were the great outspoken advocates of the ratification of the Constitution, and they were vigorously opposed by Henry, Mason, and Grayson. Marshall thus early (1788) expressed his conviction that under the proposed Constitution the Supreme Court had power to annul an act of Congress repugnant to it.[1] There

[1] Marshall in an argument before the Supreme Court at Philadelphia in the case of Ware v. Hylton, which involved the validity of a Virginia statute, defended the opposite view. "The legislative authority of any country," said he, "can only be restrained by its own municipal constitution: this is a principle that springs from the very nature of society; and the judicial authority can have no right to question the validity of law, unless such a jurisdiction is expressly given by the Constitution" (see Elliot's Debates, vol. iii., p. 553). Marshall was clearly thinking of the power of the Federal Constitution to annul a state statute. He

is no doubt that his public utterances at this time shaped his later course as Chief Justice, and that his great decision in Marbury v. Madison had its origin in beliefs held by him before he was ever thought of for the Supreme Bench.

Party conviction has been always recognized as an essential qualification for the Supreme Bench,[1] in addition to legal learning and public service. The apparent exception to this was in the offer of the Chief Justiceship to Patrick Henry by President Washington in the winter of 1795-6. Henry

---

had not yet advanced in his own thinking to this logical conclusion which he later was forced to adopt.

[1] "Looking back upon the initial controversy touching judicial functions under the Constitution, we can hardly suppose that Hamilton did not perceive that, in substance, Jefferson was right, and that a bench purposely constructed to pass upon political questions must be politically partisan. He knew well, if the Federalists prevailed in the elections, a Federalist President would only appoint magistrates who could be relied on to favor consolidation, and so the event proved. General Washington chose John Jay for the first Chief Justice who in some important respects was more Federalist than Hamilton, while John Adams selected John Marshall, who, though one of the greatest jurists who ever lived, was hated by Jefferson with a bitter hatred because of his political bias. . . . General Jackson appointed Taney to sustain the expansion of slavery, and when the antislavery party carried the country with Lincoln, Lincoln supplanted Taney with Chase, in order that Chase might stand by him in his struggle to destroy slavery. And as it has been, so must it always be. As long as the power to enact laws shall hinge on the complexion of benches or judges, so long will the ability to control a majority of the bench be as crucial a political necessity as the ability to control a majority in avowedly representative assemblies."—Brooks Adams, *The Theory of Social Revolutions* (1913), p. 53.

had been the ablest and most influential opponent of constitutional ratification in Virginia, but as Presidential Elector he supported Washington for Chief Executive, and in the meantime he had become reconciled to the provisions of the Constitution. In addition to this, he had consistently from the first commended the provisions of the Constitution relating to the judiciary. He even went so far as to express sympathy for judicial veto, declaring "it as the highest encomium on this country, that the acts of the legislature, if unconstitutional, are liable to be opposed by the judiciary."[1] Henry's peculiar interest and approval of the provisions relating to the judiciary were doubtless the determining factors in his being offered the position of Chief Justice, and such qualifications were doubtless considered in each case. Eleven[2] out of the first thirteen justices of the Supreme Court had been members of the ratification conventions in the several states, and five[3] had been members of the Constitutional Convention. Two[4] of these had declared themselves in favor of the judicial veto in the Federal Convention, and one[5] other had done so in the ratification convention in his own state. While these first twelve years of the Supreme Court were tentative and incipient in so far as results were concerned, it is easy to see that

[1] Elliot's *Debates*, vol. iii., p. 325.

[2] Jay, Rutledge, Wilson, Blair, Iredell, Johnson, Chase, Ellsworth, Cushing, Washington, and Marshall.

[3] Rutledge, Wilson, Blair, Patterson, and Ellsworth.

[4] Wilson and Ellsworth.   [5] Marshall.

only ardent supporters of a strong federal system were elevated to the Bench, and the unanimity of opinion in the early decisions had here its explanation.

In the summer of 1835, after thirty-five years of continuous service as Chief Justice, Marshall passed away at the advanced age of fourscore years. His death came during critical times, and furnished the opportunity for a decided change in the policy of the Court.   His death left a Bench of able associates, the most learned being the great Justice Story, who in legal scholarship was the equal of Marshall.   The logical thing would have been to elevate him to the Chief Justiceship. But Story's promotion was impossible, for Jackson was now serving his second term as President, and he had often found himself in opposition to the rulings of the Court, and never hesitated to ignore any of its decisions that represented views at variance with his own.   His opportunity had now come to remodel the Court after his own fashion, and the Chief Executive did not hesitate to make use of the opportunity.   Three of the five associates—McLean, Baldwin, and Wayne—held commissions signed by Jackson, and the resignation of Duval in 1836 enabled him to appoint Philip P. Barbour, of Virginia, who made the fourth.   But the real triumph of President Jackson came with his opportunity to name a Chief Justice.   He appointed Roger B. Taney of Maryland.   His political views and public conduct were in perfect harmony with those of the President. He had entered Jackson's cabinet as Attorney-General of the United States in 1831, and in this position he had taken a prominent part in the Nullification controversy, the opposition to the re-chartering of the United States Bank, the tariff, and the sub-treasury. When Mr. Duane, the Secretary of the Treasury, refused to remove the Government deposits from the Bank, Jackson promptly removed him, and appointed Taney as Secretary of the Treasury, a position which he accepted, and his first official act was to remove the bank deposits. Clay labored to defeat the nomination of Taney for Chief Justice, and made a bitter speech in opposition to his confirmation by the Senate. As we might expect with the elevation of Taney to the Chief Justiceship and the majority of his associates appointees of Jackson, a great change came in the direction and emphasis of judicial decrees. Larger emphasis was given to the rights of the states, and centralization in government was no longer proclaimed with its former vigor from the Supreme Bench.

The influence of the political views of the new Chief Justice and his associates, one of whom appeared on the Bench with him for the first time—Justice Barbour,—was soon to be manifested in judicial opinions. At the time of the death of Chief Justice Marshall there were three cases pending which involved the question of the constitutionality of state laws. These had been

argued before the Court, and Justice Story asserted that Marshall had expressed the view that
each law was unconstitutional. But as no opinion
had been handed down before the death of Marshall, it became necessary to re-argue these cases,
and it was soon found that the view of the Court
would now be different.

The first case was that of the Mayor of the
City of New York v. Miln,[1] which involved the
constitutionality of an act of the New York State
Assembly, which required the master of every
vessel arriving in the port of New York to report
in writing his passenger list, and imposing a
penalty for non-compliance. Although it was
argued that the statute was obnoxious to the
Constitution because in violation of that provision of the Constitution that gave Congress the
power to regulate commerce, and although this
view was supported by the decisions of Gibbons
v. Ogden and Brown v. The State of Maryland,
the state law was held by the majority of the
Court to be valid, the statute being a mere regulation of police, and not an attempt to regulate
commerce. Justice Barbour delivered the opinion of the Court, and Justice Story rendered a
dissenting opinion, which up to this time had been
unusual for him.

A second departure from the doctrine of Marshall is illustrated in the case of Bristoe v. Bank
of the Commonwealth of Kentucky,[2] and the

[1] II Peters, p. 102 (1837).　　[2] II Peters, p. 257 (1837).

conclusion of the Court was in direct conflict with
the case of Craig *v.* State of Missouri, a decision
rendered by Marshall as late as 1830. The question came up over the validity of a state law em-
powering a state bank to issue bills to circulate
as money, and the question arose as to whether
these bills infringed on that provision of the Constitution which denied to the states the power to
emit bills of credit. It was held that it did not,
and that the states had the power to exercise this
function. Justice Story again dissented, and
referred to the name of Marshall—"a name never
to be pronounced without reverence"—as having
denied that state institutions had the power to
issue bank-notes.

The third example is in the case of the Charles
River Bridge *v.* The Warren Bridge,[1] a case that
is notable from the fact that it is the first expression of Chief Justice Taney on a constitutional
question, and the first case in which Daniel Webster as counsel sustained defeat on a constitutional
question before the Supreme Court. The facts
are these: A ferry from Boston to Charlestown on
the Charles River had been authorized by the
Legislature of Massachusetts, and the tolls were
to be paid to the Corporation of Harvard College.
In 1785, the Legislature authorized a bridge company to construct a bridge across the river which
took the place of the ferry, and the company
agreed to pay to Harvard College an annual rental

[1] II Peters, p. 420 (1837).

for a definite number of years, after which the
rental should cease and all profits should go to the
incorporators of the bridge company.   In 1828,
the Legislature incorporated another company,
known as the Warren Bridge Company, with
power to erect a second bridge across the river.
The older corporation sought an injunction to
prevent the erection of the bridge and the exercise
of the franchise.   The state court upheld the
validity of the law granting the right of incorporation to the Warren Bridge Company and appeal
was made to the Supreme Court of the United
States on the ground that the state had attempted
to impair the obligation of contract, as the contract
of the older company with Harvard College lacked
a number of years of expiring.   The Supreme
Court sustained the right of the state to incorporate the second bridge company.   This was in
absolute conflict with the Dartmouth College case
and the case of Fletcher v. Peck, both notable
decisions of Marshall.   For the third time, Justice
Story dissented, and this time he was joined by
Justice Thompson.   In writing to a friend (Mr.
Justice McLean), Story in commenting on this
decision said: "There will not, I fear, ever in our
day be any case in which a state law or Act of
Congress will be declared unconstitutional; for
the old constitutional doctrines are fast fading
away, and a change has come over the public
mind from which I augur little good."

The climax of the judicial career of Chief

Justice Taney came with the Dred Scott decision which was handed down on March 6, 1857. The details of this famous case are too well known to require review here. This decision by the court of last resort finally resulted in an appeal to arms which was destined to reverse the decree of the nation's highest court of law. The Civil War was now at hand, and it is remarkable and interesting that during the period covered by the War no echo of it was reflected from the Supreme Court. The only change that the War produced was in the resignation of Justice Campbell, who left the Bench to devote his efforts to the cause of the South.

In 1862, the Prize Cases arose, in which the Supreme Court upheld the President's right to institute a blockade. These decisions were of preëminent importance to the cause of the North. The President had appointed three new justices— Swayne, Miller, and Davis—whose selection made these decisions possible. The attitude of the Chief Justice was clearly indicated by his decision from the Circuit Bench in the Merryman case in which he denied the right of President Lincoln to suspend the Act of Habeas Corpus. But the career of Justice Taney was about at an end. He was unable to serve on the Bench during 1863, and in October of the following year he died. On the sixth of December, 1864, Chase was appointed to succeed him.

The new Chief Justice held views also at wide

variance to those of his predecessor. He held pronounced views in opposition to slavery, and in 1841 he became one of the leaders of the Liberty Party. The fact that many of his acts while Secretary of the Treasury during the early years of the War were unconstitutional, did not deter him as Chief Justice from reverting to principles of interpretation established by Marshall. The important case of The State of Texas v. White (discussed elsewhere in this book) is sufficient illustration of the influence of party action upon judicial opinion.

Political influence was held responsible for the reversal by the Supreme Court of the decision in the case of Hepburn v. Griswold, one of the Legal Tender Cases. This case was first argued in 1869, and on the seventh of February, 1870, the Court handed down its decision declaring the Legal Tender acts unconstitutional, and that Congress had no power to make mere promises to pay dollars a legal tender in the payment of debts. President Grant, Judge Hoar, his Attorney-General, and many prominent Republicans were opposed to the conclusion reached in this case. The Court at this time consisted of eight judges, the Chief Justice and seven associates. The Chief Justice (Chase) and four associates concurred, and three dissented from the opinion. By the provisions of an act of Congress which took effect on the first Monday in December, 1869, it was enacted that "the court should consist of a chief justice and eight associates, and that, for the purpose of this act, there should be appointed an additional judge." Justice Grier, who had voted with the majority in this case, resigned February 1, 1870. President Grant, under the provisions of the judiciary act of 1869, appointed to the Supreme Bench Justices Strong and Bradley. When the case of Hepburn *v.* Griswold came up for rehearing, both of these new justices voted for reversal, which gave a majority of one. The Court and President Grant were severely criticized, but in later years the new decision has been more generally approved.

The Supreme Court remained comparatively free from party criticism from 1870 to the time it rendered the income tax decision in May, 1895. This decision was arrived at by a vote of five to four, and reversed the decision of 1880. The later decision was severely condemned by the Democratic and the Populist platforms of 1896. The Supreme Court was derided as the ally of the rich, and the defender of special privilege. There has been a growing tendency since that time to criticize the Court. Several reasons account for this condition. In the first place, the decisions of the Court are so often rendered by a divided Court, often by a five to four vote, and the diversity of grounds on which the various members have reached their diverging conclusions has suggested that the justices are prompted by party convictions rather than established and infallible guiding principles of law. Again, the decisions in the

Insular Cases and the decisions growing out of the Inter-State Commerce Act have carried loose construction to its ultimate limit. This has resulted in wide, popular criticism of the Court. The Democratic Platform of 1904 criticized the Court in this vigorous language: "It (the Republican party) forced strained and unnatural constructions upon statutes" by virtue of its control of the judiciary. Brooks Adams in his most recent book,[1] offers this explanation for the increased criticism of our courts:

"Not only has constant judicial interference dislocated scientific legislation, but casting the judiciary into the vortex of civil faction has degraded it in the popular esteem. In fine, from the outset, the American bench, because it deals with the most fiercely contested of political issues, has been an instrument necessary to political success. Consequently, political parties have striven to control it, and therefore the bench has always had an avowed partisan bias. This avowed political or social bias, has, I infer, bred among the American people the conviction that justice is not administered indifferently to all men, wherefore the bench is not respected with us as, for instance, it is in Great Britain, where law and politics are sundered. Nor has the dissatisfaction engendered by these causes been concealed. On the contrary, it has found expression through a series of famous popular leaders from Thomas Jefferson to Theodore Roosevelt."

[1] *Theory of Social Revolutions* (1913), p. 47.

The climax of opposition to the courts came in
1912, when the recall of judicial decisions[1] became
a national issue. This theory may be said to be
the direct result of opposition to the doctrine that
the courts have the power to declare a statute
unconstitutional, a doctrine that has been upheld
by the courts even from Colonial days, and was
early accepted by the Supreme Court. The
history of this doctrine will be traced in the
following chapter, as it is fundamental to the
later chapters of the book.

[1] This theory is discussed in Chapter viii.

2

CHAPTER I

JUDICIAL POWER OVER LEGISLATIVE ENACTMENTS

THE unique characteristic of the judicial department of the United States Government and the provision of the United States Constitution which more than any other has attracted attention among foreign students of political science, is the inherent power of the Federal judiciary to declare unconstitutional the enactments of the legislative branch of our Government. Much has been written on the sources of the Constitution of the United States. One author declares that "The lessons and experiences of four continents and thirty centuries lent their aid to the formation of our Federal Constitution."[1] But the power to declare a statute of a sovereign legislative body null and void has never been possessed by the courts of any European Government, and it is therefore an original feature in our judicial system. "This entrusting to the judiciary the whole interpretation of the fundamental instrument of government," says Fiske, "is the most peculiarly American feature of the work done by the convention, and to the stability of

[1] *Putney on Constitutional Law*, p. 103.

such a federation as ours, covering as it does the greater part of a huge continent, it was absolutely indispensable."[1] A consideration of this unique judicial power is fundamental to a discussion of the relation of the judiciary to political theory, for the effectiveness of political theory can only be made possible when it finds expression in legislative enactments, and, as it is the function of the courts to review the constitutionality of these legislative enactments, indirectly the judiciary passes upon political theory. It is for this reason that the courts under our Federal system have become the subject themselves, from time to time, of political debate and the center of party controversy. But it should be stated in the beginning that the courts have remained strikingly free from partisanship. However, it cannot be denied that the members of the Supreme Court have been more or less swayed by political opinion and party belief, and these opinions have to some extent, at least, been reflected in the opinions rendered from the Bench.

Judicial power to interpret political theory is a latent force until the theory is enacted into law, and the law invoked as a means of remedial justice. Generally speaking, every law that is the result of a political issue before the people, previous to, or at the time of, its enactment, becomes, sooner or later, in some form a subject for judicial review. This process is becoming more and more the man-

[1] Fiske, *The Critical Period of American History*, p. 301.

ner in which the party opposing the issue tests the soundness of the principle underlying it, and the degree to which the law conforms to the issue. The judiciary may assume three attitudes toward a statute: First, it may simply make a remark about a law without supporting or condemning it in any way. It is not always necessary for an appellate court or a court of last resort to pass upon the merits of a law, appeals often being taken upon other grounds; and it has been the usual policy of the courts to adhere to this policy. The most violent criticism offered to the Dred Scott decision was that in passing upon the merits of the Missouri Compromise the Court was passing upon a question not properly before the Court. Secondly, it may be to maintain the constitutionality of the law, in which case it usually becomes the settled policy of the land, subject, of course, to modification or extension, within definite constitutional limits, by Congress. The most prominent exception was the Missouri Compromise, in which the people refused to accept the verdict of the Supreme Court. The third attitude may be that of declaring the statute unconstitutional and thereby reversing the theory on which the law was based, annulling a cherished view of the majority, and supporting the wisdom of the minority. This is such a remarkable power and so unusual in governmental science as to merit a rather extended discussion as to its history, extent, and limitation in our country.

The two great law systems from which we have drawn most largely never recognized this power in their courts. This statement has been partially denied by one or two authorities. In the very scholarly work of Brinton Coxe[1] it is maintained that there were probably three doctrines in the civil law of Rome on which this American judicial theory might be based. He held that "Jus Legum" was considered the fundamental act in organic law, an example of which was the Cæcilia et Didia, which was a law that prohibited the proposal of any enactment which contained unrelated provisions, the design of which was to prevent omnibus legislation and had for its purpose the prevention of a statute having more than one subject. Mr. Coxe cites as a concrete example a reference in one of the orations of Cicero concerning Clodius, in which he proclaims to his hearers that the Senate had annulled the laws of Marcus Drusus because they had violated this rule. Another instance cited by this learned author, in substantiation of his theory, was certain provisions of the code of Justinian, in which he claimed that the judges were enjoined to treat as invalid a rescript of the Emperor, which was contrary to established law, or that had been illegally obtained. The third provision referred to mandates, or power of attorney, in cases where an agent exceeded his authority, all such being without effect

[1] *Judicial Power and Unconstitutional Legislation*, or Appendix H, p. 323 of Howe's *Studies in the Civil Law*.

and void. But the student who investigates the passages referred to by Mr. Coxe is forced to believe that his theory is based on slim foundations and that his view is entirely erroneous. It is easy to determine the Roman doctrine from *Lex Siete Partidas*, which is the most important code of the Middle Ages, and a direct descendant of the civil law of Rome: "When doubts arise concerning the meaning of law, whether from an error in committing it to writing, or from the obscurity of the expressions made use of by the legislators, *it belongs to the legislature alone to explain such doubts.*" [1]

Under the Roman law system the pontiffs interpreted the law and applied it to special conditions, but they had no power to annul the decrees of the Senate. When the Twelve Tables became the foundation of Roman law, the pontiffs still continued to be for a long period the only judges, but under these laws they were restricted to their provisions. When the office of prætor was created in 366 B.C. to interpret the law, no power was given to them to annul the decrees of the Senate, of the *comitia centuriata*, or the Emperor, the respective dominating sources of law in the future history of Rome. The question of the power of the pontiffs and prætors to annul established law seems never to have been seriously considered by the Roman jurisprudents. This may have been largely due to the fact that Roman legislation was principally

[1] *Lex Siete Partidas*, Partido I., Title L., Law 14.

concerned with substantive law, leaving the adjective law to the prætors, who were entirely responsible for the formulary system. During the best days of the Empire, imperial legislation was somewhat influenced by the jurisconsults, who were the literary and philosophic lawyers of their times, and as a result of their learning, they were often consulted by the Emperor; but after a decree had been issued it passed beyond the control of any governmental agency except that of the Emperor himself.

In England, as in early Rome, the earliest legislation was merely a royal decree, and the King being a legislative and judicial officer as well as the executive, there could be no conflict of authority. But in England the supremacy of the legislative act was recognized as soon as there was a shadow of a legislative body. Stubbs says:[1]

"The legislative functions of the national council are, under the Norman kings, rather nominal than real. But the form of participation is retained; it is still with the counsel and consent of his faithful that Henry the First amends, as his father had done, the old laws. This immemorial counsel and consent descends from the earliest Teutonic legislation, and is preserved to our day, a standing and perpetual protest against the imperial doctrine favored by the lawyers and founded on the devolution of all legislative power on the King—*Quod principi placuit legis habet vigorem.*"

[1] *Select Charters*, p. 17.

The Revolution of 1688 effectively transferred the principle of sovereignty from the King to Parliament. This transfer was the historical outgrowth of the increasing exercise of legislative power in a country without a written constitution. Even the source of power in Parliament has shifted in the course of history. The Lords, who were the natural successors of the great council, became the Parliament, and exercised supreme power for a time.[1] The elective assembly finally gained supremacy, and assumed supreme sovereignty. Bagehot[2] tells us that not only is the supreme authority under the English Constitution vested in the House of Commons, but more particularly in each succeeding *newly-elected* House of Commons.

Blackstone,[3] writing of a later period, has more positively declared the English doctrine as follows:

"An act of Parliament is the exercise of the highest authority that this kingdom acknowledges upon earth. It has power to bind every subject of the land and the dominions thereunto belonging; nay, even the King himself, if particularly named therein. And it cannot be altered, amended, dispensed with, suspended, or repealed but in the same forms and by the same authority of Parliament."

A few ineffectual attempts have been made by the English judiciary to modify this doctrine.

[1] Hume's *History of England*, vol. i., p. 453.
[2] The *English Constitution*, p. 295.   [3] Vol. i., pp. 185–6.

Mr. Coxe contends that there were in England, prior to 1688, a few cases where the judges seemed to believe themselves possessed with power to annul the acts of Parliament. He claims that in Rous *v.* An Abbott, 27 Henry VI., a statute was held void. He claims also that in Prior of Castlaker *v.* Dean, 21 Henry VII., where an act of Parliament was designed to make a king a parson, the act was held to be void, because in violation of the cannon law which was regarded as a part of the English Constitution. Again in the case of Godden *v.* Hales, the King's Bench in 1788 held that certain provisions in the statute of 25 Charles II., chap. 2, were null and void, because they infringed upon a prerogative of the King which was constitutional. It is thought by the learned author who cites these cases that this was an attempt to adopt into the English law system the fragments of the doctrine which he claimed to find in the civil law system. But probably, if the English judges ever conceived that they had the power to annul statute of Parliament, their belief grew out of their great respect for the common law rather than from any analogy they might have discovered in the Roman system. So great a judge as Lord Coke, out of deference to the common law, asserted that those acts of Parliament contrary to reason should be subservient to the common law. Coke says:

"And it appears in our books that in many cases the common law will control acts of parliament, and sometimes adjudge them to be utterly void; for when an act of parliament is against the common right or reason and repugnant or impossible to be performed, the common law will control it and adjudge such act to be void."[1]

However, this natural justice theory of Coke never took deep root in English judicial soil.

In France it seems that legislative supremacy was one of the products of the French Revolution. The assembling of the States General in May, 1789, gave an opportunity for the Third Estate to gain control of the legislative machinery, and they assumed as their primary business the making of a new constitution after organizing themselves into the National Assembly. These men had experienced hardships because of an absolute executive, and it was but natural that this body would make the legislative branch of the Government superior to the executive branch, and to make this superiority doubly sure it was but natural that they should also provide that the legislature should not have its decrees suspended or annulled by the courts. The Constituent Assembly, therefore, provided that "the tribunals shall not participate directly or indirectly in the exercise of the legislative power, nor interfere with or suspend the execution of the decrees of the legislative body sanctioned by the king under

[1] *Bonham's Case*, 4th Rep.; Part viii., p. 234.

pain of forfeiture of their offices." This principle has been strictly adhered to in France to the present day. Dicey[1] says that

"Any one who bears in mind the respect paid in France from the time of the Revolution onwards to the legislation of *de facto* governments and the traditions of the French judicature will assume with confidence that an enactment passed through the Chambers, promulgated by the President, and published in the *Bulletin des Lois* will be held valid by every tribunal throughout the republic."

The American doctrine has never been recognized in the German Empire. In Germany, the courts are required to enforce without question the legislative will, repugnancy to the constitution offers no excuse to do otherwise. The German theory is expressed by Garner[2] as follows:

"It is not their (the court's) right to assume that the Legislature, intentionally or unwittingly, has exceeded its powers; not their prerogative to set aside as invalid what has been enacted, presumably after careful deliberation and with full knowledge of its own constitutional powers."

The other nations of Europe subscribe to the doctrine of legislative supremacy. Belgium, Italy, and Spain have followed the example of France. The Constitution of the Confederacy of Switzer-

[1] *Law of the Constitution*, p. 122 (Second Edition).
[2] *Introduction to Political Science*, p. 597.

land makes it mandatory upon the part of the courts to give full force and effect to every law enacted by the Federal Assembly. So, we may call this a European doctrine as distinguished from the American doctrine that the courts have the power to annul an enactment of the Legislature deemed by them to be repugnant to some provision of the Constitution.

"In Europe," says Esmein,[1] "and especially under the régime of imperative and written constitutions, the idea is well established that the tribunals have no right to pass upon the constitutionality of the laws. When regularly enacted they are binding upon the courts, and they have only the right to apply them, not to judge of their validity."

In striking contrast with European practice, the American courts began at a very early date to exercise the authority of declaring statute laws unconstitutional when it was believed that such law contravened the Constitution. It is natural to seek the source of such a practice. As we have seen, a precedent could scarcely be found in the practices of any European country. However, there may have been the seed of suggestion in the decisions of the English courts referred to above, and they doubtless did find judicial soil in which to grow in the early days of our colonial history.

[1] *Droit Constitution*, p. 431. Also quoted by Garner in *Introduction to Political Science*, p. 597.

For in the colonies appeal was often taken to the King, and the English courts frequently annulled acts of the colonial legislatures on the ground that they exceeded the authority granted to them in the colonial charter. It was doubtless in this way that the judicial power to declare legislative acts unconstitutional gradually grew up in our governmental system. No colonial charter ever expressly delegated this power to the courts. This doctrine has never been incorporated in the Constitution of the United States, or in any of the constitutions of the states of the American Union. The acceptance of this all-important generalization is the result of its consistent and frequent reaffirmation by the courts through a long period of time.

The earliest case we have which supported this doctrine was that of Robin *v.* Hardaway,[1] a Virginia case, decided in 1772. This was an action brought by the descendants of an enslaved Indian woman, in which they sought to secure their freedom. They contended that the enabling statute under which they were deprived of their freedom was invalid, because it was contrary to natural right and justice. The plaintiff's counsel, George Mason, cited Lord Coke and other authorities in support of the following declaration:

"Now, all acts of the Legislature apparently contrary to natural right and justice are, in our laws,

[1] Jeff. 109.

and must be in the nature of things, considered void. The laws of nature are the laws of God, whose authority can be superseded by no power on earth. A Legislature must not obstruct our obedience to Him from whose punishment they cannot protect us. All human constitutions which contradict His laws we are in conscience bound to disobey.''

This case was decided on other grounds, and the Court did not deem it necessary to discuss this point. But we have revealed here the transplanted doctrine of Lord Coke, which was destined in the course of our history to show much vitality. However, it was not to develop from the broad premise announced here, but on the more restricted ground of the limitation of powers given to our Federal Legislature by the Constitution.

Ten years after the argument in the case cited above, the remarkable decision in the case of Commonwealth *v.* Caton was rendered. This was also a Virginia case. Two questions were at issue, as follows: (1) Whether under the constitution of Virginia the house of burgesses could legally grant a pardon for treason; (2) Whether the definition of treason in an act of 1776, and under which a number of convictions was secured, was in violation of the state constitution. It happened that the decision did not turn upon the constitutionality of the act, and, therefore, the remarks of the judges are merely *obiter dicta.* However, the expressions used are the first to be found relating directly to the subject. Judge Wythe, in asserting the controlling powers of the courts and after reviewing the circumstances of the case, declared that he would feel it to be his duty to prevent the usurpations by one branch of the Legislature of rights belonging to the other, and concluded with this remarkable language:

" Nay, more, if the whole Legislature—an event to be deprecated—should attempt to overleap the boundaries prescribed to them by the people, I, in administering the justice of the country, will meet the united powers at my seat in this tribunal, and pointing to the Constitution, will say to them, 'Here is the limit of your authority; hither shall you go, but no further.' "

Judge Pendleton, the President of the Court, refrained from expressing a direct opinion, but his remarks are significant.

" But how far this Court in whom the judiciary powers may, in some sort, be said to be concentrated, shall have power to declare the nullity of a law passed in its forms by the legislative power, without exercising the power of that branch contrary to the plain terms of the Constitution, is indeed a deep, important, and, I will add, tremendous question, the decision of which might involve consequences to which gentlemen may not have extended their ideas."[1]

[1] See Carson's, *The History of the Supreme Court of the United States*, vol. i., p. 121; also Reives' *Life of Madison*, vol. ii., p. 262 *et seq.*

It was the opinion of the other judges, including Chancellor Blair, so we are told, that the Court possessed the power to annul a resolution or an act of the Legislature if in conflict with the Constitution.

It must not be inferred that this doctrine was always accepted without protest on the part of the people of the colonies. In some of the colonies, it is true, the doctrine came in so gradually and was announced in connection with matters of such small commercial importance as to arouse but little comment or antagonism. But the opposite effect was also produced. Bryce[1] cites a case in point:

" In 1786 the Supreme Court of Rhode Island decided that an act passed by the Legislature was unconstitutional because it contravened the provision of the colonial charter (which was still the constitution of the state), securing to every accused person the benefit of a trial by jury. The Legislature was furious and proceeded to impeach the judges for disobeying their will. The impeachment failed, but the judges were not reëlected by the Legislature when their term of office expired."

The agitation of this question in some of the colonies just before the Federal convention met caused discussion in the convention as to the advisability of giving the Federal judiciary power to annul acts of Congress which were deemed repugnant to the Constitution. Charles Pinckney

[1] The *American Commonwealth*, vol. i., p. 533.

opposed giving the judges this power, because, by the very nature of our Government, the judges would be involved in party conflicts before coming to the Bench, and their political views would tinge their decisions later in court. "The judiciary," said John Francis Mercer, of Maryland, "ought to be separate from the legislature and independent of it. I disapprove the doctrine that the judges should, as expositors of the Constitution, have authority to declare a law void. Laws ought to be well and cautiously made, and then to be uncontrollable."[1] This was part of the Anti-Federalist argument used against the adoption of the Constitution by the States. Against this view was that of Hamilton and Marshall. Hamilton thought the people needed to give the courts such a power to protect them from obscure or equivocal laws, "for," said he, "all new laws, though penned with the greatest technical skill, and passed on the fullest and most mature deliberation, are considered more or less obscure and equivocal until their meaning be liquidated and ascertained by a series of particular discussions and adjudications."[2] Again Hamilton says:

" There is no position which depends on clearer principles, than that every act of a delegated authority, contrary to the tenor of the commission under which it is exercised, is void. No legis-

[1] See on this point Bancroft's *History of the Constitution of the United States*, p. 349.
[2] *Federalist Paper*, No. 36 (Dawson's Edition).

3

34 Interpretation of Political Theory

lative act, therefore, contrary to the Constitution,
can be valid. To deny this, would be to affirm
that the deputy is greater than his principal; that
the servant is above his master; that the representatives of the people are superior to the people
themselves; that men acting by virtue of powers,
may do not only what their powers do not authorize, but what they forbid. . . . The interpretation of the laws is the proper and peculiar province
of the courts. A Constitution is, in fact, and
must be regarded by the judges, as a fundamental
law. It therefore belongs to them to ascertain
its meaning, as well as the meaning of any particular act proceeding from the legislative body.
If there should happen to be an irreconcilable
variance between the two, that which has the
superior obligation and validity ought, of course,
to be preferred; or in other words, the Constitution ought to be preferred to the statute; the
intention of the people to the intention of their
agents."[1]

It was thought by this means legislation could
be kept within the bounds of the Constitution.
Marshall emphasized this point in his defense of
the Constitution before the Virginia convention,
on June 10, 1788. He said:

"If they (Congress) were to make a law not war-
ranted by any of the powers enumerated, it would
be considered by the judges as an infringement of
the Constitution which they are to guard. They
would not consider such a law as coming under
their jurisdiction. They would declare it void."

[1] *Federalist Paper*, No. 78 (Dawson's Edition).

The Constitution does not expressly give to the courts the power to declare statutes unconstitutional; but the defenders of the Constitution, before its ratification, seem to have assumed that such a power was given from the wording of Article III., section 2.

The first of a large number of decisions asserting the power of the state courts to declare a statute void because in conflict with the Constitution of the United States was that of Holmes *v*. Walton, a New Jersey case, and decided by the Supreme Court of that State. The statute in controversy declared that under the seizure laws trial should be by a jury consisting of six men, and objection was made that this was not a constitutional jury. The Court took this view of the question and held the statute to be void. A little later, another statute was held to be unconstitutional, in the same State, because held to be *ex post facto* and therefore in conflict with the Constitution of the United States. It seems that these decisions met with no opposition from the Legislature or the people, for the Legislature promptly accepted the views of the Court in the first case, and changed the statute so as to provide for a jury of twelve men instead of six. The power of the state judiciary to measure state statutes by the Federal Constitution was not destined to be accepted in all the states with the equanimity that characterized the enunciation of the doctrine in New Jersey. In the states of Ohio, Kentucky, and Pennsylvania the doctrine was contested with much vigor. Cooley[1] cites an Ohio instance in 1807 where impeachment proceedings were instituted against the judges who upheld the doctrine, but without effecting their removal from office. The people of Ohio seem to have accepted the doctrine after the failure to remove the judges from office, for, in 1829, the Supreme Court of Ohio reiterated the doctrine in the case of Jordon v. Dayton.[2]   At this time no opposition was raised and it is presumed that it had been generally acceded to by the people. In Kentucky the affirmation of this doctrine resulted in a bitter political contest.   One faction was called the "Old Court," and the other the "New Court," faction.   The "New Court," faction was fighting the recognition of the doctrine; while the "Old Court," was supporting it.   The latter faction was finally sustained by the people and the Court decision which they had made an issue was given recognition.

. The Federal courts were not long in asserting the doctrine.   The first case involving the doctrine grew out of a statute passed by Congress and considered in March, 1792.   This statute provided for adjusting the claims of widows and orphans barred by limitation previously established, and regulating the claims to invalid pensions.   United States courts were directed to pass upon the

[1] *Constitutional Limitations*, p. 193 (Sixth Edition).
[2] 4 *Ohio*, p. 294.

claims subject to the review and approval of the Secretary of War as well as by Congress.

The statute was reviewed by the Circuit Court for the District of New York, over which Justice Jay presided. The part of the opinion in point reads as follows:

"The duties assigned to the Circuit Court by this act are not judicial insomuch as it subjects the decision of these courts, made pursuant to those duties, first to the consideration and supervision of the Secretary of War, and then to the revision of the legislature; whereas by the Constitution, neither the Secretary of War, nor any other executive officer, nor even the legislature are authorized to sit as a court of errors on the judicial acts or the opinions of this court. But, as the objects of this act are exceedingly benevolent and do real honor to the humanity and justice of Congress; and as the judges desire to manifest on all proper occasions and in every proper way, their high respect for the National Legislature, they will execute this act *in the capacity of commissioners.*"

A view of this statute was also expressed by the Circuit Court for the District of Pennsylvania.

The historic development, as well as the extent to which the courts should logically carry the doctrine, was set forth in a learned decision by Justice Iredell, in the case of Calder *v.* Bull.[1] The question at issue grew out of a Connecticut law which was claimed to be *ex post facto*, and, therefore, unconstitutional. Without reviewing the merits

[1] 3 Dallas, 386.

of the case, I simply quote the language touching the point under discussion. After considering the supreme power of Parliament, the Court said,

"In order, therefore, to guard against an evil, it has been the policy of all the American states which have, individually, framed their state constitutions since the Revolutionary War, and the people of the United States when they framed the Federal Constitution, to define with precision the objects of the legislative power, and to restrain its exercise within marked and settled boundaries. If any act of Congress, or of the Legislature of a state, violates those constitutional provisions, it is unquestionably void; though, I admit, that as the authority to declare it void is of a delicate and awful nature, the Court will never resort to that authority, but in a clear and urgent case. If, on the other hand, the Legislature of the Union, or the Legislature of any member of the Union, shall pass a law, within the scope of their constitutional power, the Court cannot pronounce it to be void, merely because it is, in their judgment, contrary to the principles of natural justice. The ideas of natural justice are regulated by no fixed standard; the ablest and purest men have differed upon the subject; and all that the Court could possibly say, in such an event, would be, that the Legislature, possessed of an equal right of opinion, had passed an act which, in the opinion of the judges, was inconsistent with the abstract principles of justice."

The effect of this decision was to give judicial limitation to the argument of counsel in the early

Virginia case of Robin *v.* Hardeman, that the courts should measure the legality of a statute by the standards of abstract justice; but this decision, in unequivocal terms, affirms that the courts have the right to measure a statute by the terms and import of the Constitution. Undoubtedly this decision had much weight as a precedent, but the opinion in the case of Marbury *v.* Madison was the one that settled the doctrine in the Federal courts.

This case, reported in 1 Cranch, 137, was submitted to the Supreme Court in 1803. Marbury held a judicial appointment under John Adams, which had been duly approved by the Senate, his commission was duly signed and sealed, but not delivered. Before Marbury could begin his duties, Adams was superseded by Madison as President, who refused to deliver the commission. Marbury applied to the Supreme Court for a writ of mandamus to compel the delivery of the commission. The decision sustained the contention of Marbury. But in doing so, the justices held that that clause of the Judiciary Act that gave the Supreme Court original jurisdiction in issuing writs of mandamus was unconstitutional; hence, inoperative and void. The decision is too long to quote here, but substantially the Court held that supreme sovereignty resides in the people. They have the power to organize the Government and to assign to the different departments their respective powers. They have the authority to define the ultimate

power of each. The Constitution defined the
limits of legislative power, and beyond these limits
Congress could not go without the expressed will
of the people in the form of constitutional amendments. It was to be definitely understood that
under our written Constitution Congress did not
possess, and could not exercise, the omnipotence
of Parliament. The courts are compelled in the
exercise of their official functions to recognize
this limitation of Congress. The courts cannot
give force and effect to legislative acts that attempt to bestow privileges or grant rights that
the Constitution forbids. Such an act of Congress, repugnant to the Constitution, is void; and it
is clearly the duty and the essence of judicial
power to so decree. For the courts to fail in the
performance of this important duty would result
in reducing the Constitution to the level with the
ordinary acts of the Legislature. This, of course,
was not contemplated or desired, either by the
framers of the Constitution, or the people who
ratified it. The Constitution was accepted by
the people with the understanding that it was to
be the " superior, paramount law, and unchangeable by ordinary means." The courts are compelled to take cognizance of this fact. They must
weigh every law in the constitutional balance, and
if the law falls short, the courts must so declare.
If both the statute and the Constitution apply to a
particular case, and these are in conflict, it is clearly
the duty of the court to uphold the Constitution,

and to declare the statute void. Those, then, who controvert the principle that the Constitution is to be considered, in Court, as a paramount law, are reduced to the necessity of maintaining that courts must close their eyes on the Constitution, and see only the law. "No person," says the Constitution, "shall be convicted of treason unless on the testimony of two witnesses to the same overt act, or on confession in open Court." Here the language is addressed directly to the Court. It prescribes a rule of evidence not to be departed from. If the Legislature should change this rule, and declare one witness, or a confession out of Court, sufficient for a conviction, must the constitutional principle yield to the legislative act? It is apparent that the framers of the Constitution contemplated that instrument as a rule for the government of courts, as well as of the Legislature. Judges in their official oaths swear to discharge the duties of their office agreeably to the Constitution and the laws of the United States. Why does a judge swear to discharge his duties agreeably to the Constitution of the United States if that Constitution forms no rule for his government—if it is closed upon him and cannot be inspected by him? If such be the real state of things, this is worse than solemn mockery. To prescribe or take this oath becomes equally a crime. A few extracts from this historic opinion will illustrate the remorseless logic of the great Chief Justice.

"The question whether an act repugnant to the Constitution can become the law of the land, is a question deeply interesting to the United States, but happily not of an intricacy proportioned to its interest. It seems only necessary to recognize certain principles supposed to have been long and well-established to decide it. . . . The powers of the Legislature are defined and limited; and that those limits may not be mistaken or forgotten, the Constitution is written. . . . The Constitution is either a superior paramount law, unchangeable by ordinary means, or it is on a level with ordinary legislative acts, and, like other acts, is alterable when the Legislature shall please to alter it. If the former part of the alternative be true, then written Constitutions are absurd attempts, on the part of the people, to limit a power in its own nature illimitable. . . . If an act of the Legislature repugnant to the Constitution is void, does it, notwithstanding its invalidity, bind the courts, and oblige them to give it effect? Or, in other words, though it be not a law, does it constitute a rule as operative as if it were a law? This would be to overthrow in fact what was established in theory, and would seem at first view an absurdity too gross to be insisted on. It shall, however, receive a more attentive consideration. It is emphatically the province and duty of the judicial department to say what the law is. Those who apply the rule to particular cases must of necessity expound and interpret that rule. If two laws conflict with each other, the courts must decide on the operation of each. So is a law in opposition to the Constitution; if both the law and Constitution apply to a particular case, so that the Court must either decide that case conformably to the law, disregarding the Constitution, or conformably to the Constitution, disregarding the law,—the Court must determine which of these conflicting rules governs the case. This is of the very essence of judicial duty. If, then, the courts are to regard the Constitution, and the Constitution is superior to any ordinary act of the Legislature, the Constitution and not such ordinary act, must govern the case to which they both apply."[1]

The effect of this decision was practically to settle the doctrine in the Federal courts. It had, also, a tremendous weight in establishing the doctrine in the state courts. Its logic was invincible; its argument so clear as to leave little room to doubt its correctness.

Rufus Choate has said, with reference to this decision (Marbury *v.* Madison) and the importance of the doctrine, that:

"I do not know that I can point to one achievement in American statesmanship which can take rank for its consequence of good above that single decision of the Supreme Court, which adjudged an act of the Legislature contrary to the Constitution to be void, and that the judicial department is clothed with the power to ascertain the repugnancy, and pronounce the legal conclusion. That the framers of the Constitution intended this to be so is certain; but to have asserted it against Congress and the Executive, to have vindicated it by that easy, yet adamantine demonstration than

---

[1] 1 Cranch, p. 137; also quoted in Carson's *The History of the Supreme Court*, vol. i., p. 219, *et seq.*

which the reasoning of mathematics shows nothing surer, to have inscribed this vast truth of conservatism upon the public mind, so that no demagogue, not in the last stage of intoxication, denies it—this is an achievement of statesmanship (of the judiciary) of which a thousand years may not exhaust or reveal all the good."

But one link remains in the long chain of decisions to make it complete; *i. e.*, in cases where the statutes of a state are repugnant to the Constitution. The first of a long line of decisions declaring a state law void and of no effect, because it violated a principle of the Federal Constitution, is that of Fletcher *v.* Peck.[1] This decision is also historic, because it was the first judicial restriction by the Supreme Court upon the powers of the states. Of this decision Carson says:

"It towers above the decisions of a period of many years, important and imposing though they are, and, with Marbury *v.* Madison, stands as an outspur of that magnificent range of adjudications which bear to our constitutional jurisprudence the relative strength and majesty of the Rocky Mountains to our physical geography."[2]

In this case the State of Georgia had sought, by legislative enactment, to dispossess a landholder of his property, which had been acquired under a previous statute of the same state. The Supreme

[1] 6 Cranch, p. 87.
[2] *The History of the Supreme Court,* p. 219 *et seq.*

Court held that a grant thus acquired was an executed contract, and that the owner should not be dispossessed even by subsequent legislation. The Court approached the question of the unconstitutionality of the state statute in a solemn and dignified manner:

"The question whether a law be void for its repugnance to the Constitution is at all times a question of much delicacy, which ought seldom, if ever, to be decided in the affirmative in a doubtful case. The Court, when impelled by duty to render such a judgment, would be unworthy of its station could it be unmindful of the solemn obligations which that station imposes. But it is not on slight implication and vague conjecture that the Legislature is to be pronounced to have transcended its powers, and its acts to be considered as void. The opposition between the Constitution and the law should be such that the judge feels a clear and strong conviction of their incompatibility with each other."

With this decision, and thus early (1810), the power of the Supreme Court to declare a statute null and void, because repugnant to the Constitution, was now complete and the doctrine has never since been seriously controverted, for, as we have seen, the principle was maintained by the colonial courts in colonial days, it was early declared with reference to a Federal statute by our Supreme Court, and it was but a logical and natural step to reaffirm the doctrine with reference to the acts of the legislatures of the various states. With this brief review of this important doctrine, we are now to trace its application in those legislative enactments that reflect political issues. It is true, as Bryce says, "Some questions, and among them many which involve political issues, can never come before the Federal courts, because they are not such as are raisable in an action between parties"; still, most of the great political issues that have composed party doctrine have been opposed on constitutional grounds, and these, when enacted into law, have usually, in some form, become matters for judicial decree. The American doctrine of judicial supremacy itself was more or less of a political issue in the early history under our Constitution. With the settlement of this doctrine as an ill-defined issue, the foundation was laid for the final solution of all those political issues that were fundamental and vital. Some, as we shall see, were founded on sound theory, and based upon a keen insight into the nature of our political institutions; others, were to contain false doctrine, incorrect inferences, and faulty vision. Each of the two great parties, at times, has had its share of each. Both have long since recognized the advantage "of relegating questions not only intricate and delicate, but peculiarly liable to excite political passions, to the cool, dry atmosphere of judicial determination," and to accept in good faith the power of the judiciary to uphold the sound and rescind the false.

CHAPTER II

THEORY OF CONSTITUTIONAL CONSTRUCTION

COMPARATIVELY few of the numerous differences that arose in the Federal Convention were destined to remain unsettled after the adoption and ratification of the Constitution. The uncertainty as to aim at the beginning of the Convention made disagreement certain. The views as to the nature of the Government extended from a *Statenbund* on the one hand to a *Bunderstadt* on the other with every shade of view between these. The former view found expression in the Virginia plan, and the latter in the New Jersey plan. From the submission of the Virginia plan on May the 29th, until September the 17th, when the Convention finished its work, there was a constant clash of opinion, followed by compromise or concession. But with the final adoption of the Constitution, many of these differences disappeared and the delegates returned to their respective states and worked for the ratification of the Constitution. These were called Federalists and their opponents, who sought to prevent the ratification in the form submitted, were called Anti-Federalists. These parties marked the beginning of party history with reference to our Federal institutions. The Anti-Federalist party stood for the freedom of the individual citizen and the restriction of Federal interference in the affairs of the states. The most fundamental of their doctrines was that of the manner of the construction to be given this Constitution when adopted. The party name ceased to be applicable after the adoption of the Constitution, and they then began to be called Republicans or Democratic-Republicans. The history and result of the two views of construing the organic law will now be considered.

Jefferson soon became the leading advocate of strict construction and the most prominent member of the Republican party. He supported his doctrine with the ninth and tenth amendments to the Constitution, which are as follows: "The enumeration in the Constitution of certain rights shall not be construed to deny or disparage others retained by the people," and "The powers not delegated to the United States by the Constitution, nor prohibited by it to the States, are reserved to the States respectively or to the people." Hamilton, the great Federalist leader, made his maxim, "If the end is clearly defined, the means must be employed to reach it," justify his belief in the implied powers and loose construction. While there can be little doubt that strict construction was a sound principle in theory, the difficulty of amending the Constitution has led to the adoption of the principle of loose construction. In fact,

Jefferson found himself compelled to violate his cherished doctrine. The purchase of the Louisiana territory was beyond any possible expressed power granted in the Constitution. Bryce, in his *American Commonwealth*, has characterized this as "the boldest step ever taken by a President." Jefferson recognized his inconsistency and sought to have his act ratified by constitutional amendment, but the general approval of the people caused Congress to ignore the request. The Embargo Act of December 22, 1807, was passed at the instance of Jefferson, which prohibited the sailing of any merchant vessel from any American port, save coasters. Jefferson could hardly have justified this act under a policy of strict construction. The defenders of loose construction, on the other hand, were not unwilling to use Jeffersonian doctrine when their commercial interests were jeopardized. During the War of 1812, when the commercial interests began to suffer in the New England states, the Hartford Convention was held in which secession was threatened on the ground that Congress and the Executive had exceeded their authority under the Constitution.

Opposition to other early legislative measures caused widespread discussion of the limitation of the powers of Congress. Notable among these were the Alien and Sedition laws, passed by a Federalist Congress in 1798. These laws brought forth the famous Virginia and Kentucky Resolutions, which Woodburn[1] calls "the first party

[1] *Political Parties and Party Problems*, p. 18.

4

platform ever published in America." Judicial
power was not invoked to pass upon the constitutionality of these laws. The general opposition
of the people caused their early repeal. It is
interesting to contemplate what might have been
the result had these laws been passed upon by
the Supreme Court and adversely decided before
Marshall came to the Bench.

The doctrine of loose construction has had party
support from the earliest days of our history, and
the Democratic party has opposed it from the
days of Jefferson until now. It was not the
custom in our early political history to adopt
platforms and hold conventions,[1] but well-
defined views existed upon this subject. When
the convention system began and the custom
was established of submitting a party platform,
the demand for strict construction was an
early declaration of the Democratic party. In
their platform of 1840 the following language
was used:

"Resolved, that the Federal Government is one
of limited powers, derived solely from the Constitution, and the grants of power shown therein ought
to be strictly construed by all the departments and
agents of the Government, and that it is inexpedient and dangerous to exercise doubtful constitutional powers."

[1] The first formal platform ever adopted was issued by the
National Republicans in May of 1832, and presidential candidates
were first nominated by conventions in that year.

This doctrine has been reiterated in practically every platform from that time to this. In most cases the language of this first declaration has been used. In the platform of 1880, after pledging anew their allegiance to the constitutional doctrines and traditions of the Democratic party, the plank that follows "declares opposition to centralization and the spirit of encroachments." Most of the platforms since that time have used the word "centralization" in describing the danger to which the country is subjected under a policy of loose construction. The Whigs, in their platform of 1852, also adopted this Democratic doctrine and voiced it in the following words: "The Government of the United States is of a limited character, and is confined to the exercise of powers especially granted by the Constitution."

This important question has been at the bottom of most of the differences that have become issues between the dominating parties of the country. Very few of the leading decisions of the Supreme Court on constitutional questions have failed to incorporate into its argument the Court's views upon the subject of the manner of construing the Constitution. The attitude of the Supreme Court upon the question is one of unusual interest and importance. The view-point is novel in governmental science, because under no other constitutional government could this question arise. The doctrine will now be traced as briefly as possible through the decisions of the Supreme Court.

The earliest case touching upon this question was that of the United States *v.* Fisher.[1] This was a decision construing an act of March, 1797, in which a preference was given to the United States in cases of insolvency. Upon this point the Court said:

"The preference claimed by the United States is not prohibited; but it has been truly said that under a constitution conferring specific powers, the power contended for must be granted, or it cannot be exercised. It is claimed under the authority to make all laws which shall be necessary and proper to carry into execution the powers vested by the Constitution in the Government of the United States, or in any department or officer thereof. In construing this clause it would produce endless difficulties if the opinion should be maintained that no law was authority which was indispensably necessary to give effect to a specific power."

This opinion finds its justification for tending toward loose construction in the last paragraph of Section VIII., Article I.

The next step in the development of the doctrine was in a very carefully considered opinion delivered by Justice Story.[2] This emphatic language was used:

"The Government of the United States can claim no powers which are not granted to it by the Con-

[1] 2 Cranch, 496.
[2] Martin *v.* Hunters Lessee, 1 Wheaton, 560.

stitution and the powers actually granted must be such as are expressly given, or given by necessary implication. On the other hand, this instrument, like every other grant, is to have a reasonable construction, according to the import of the terms; and where a power is expressly given in general terms, it is to be restrained to particular cases, unless the construction grows out of the context expressly or by necessary implication. The Constitution, unavoidably, deals in general language. It did not suit the purposes of the people, in framing this great charter of our liberties, to provide for minute specifications of its powers, or to declare the means by which those powers should be carried into execution. It was foreseen that this would be a perilous and difficult, if not an impossible, task. The instrument was not intended for the exigencies of a few years, but was to endure through a long lapse of ages, the events of which were locked up in the inscrutable purposes of Providence. It could not be foreseen what new changes and modifications of power might be indispensable to effectuate the general object of the charter; and restrictions and specifications, which at the present might seem salutary, might, in the end, prove the overthrow of the system itself. Hence, its powers are expressed in general terms, leaving to the legislature, from time to time, to adopt its own means to effectuate legitimate objects, and to mold and model the exercise of its powers, as its own wisdom and the public interest should require."

This decision was rendered during the February term of 1816, and it has been considered one of the most important that the Supreme Court has rendered. For in addition to the question above, the decision took advanced ground on the question of the nature of the Federal Union, which was to become such a vital issue a generation later. The doctrine announced above as to legislative power has recently brought forth a notable utterance from President Taft, leader of the party that has stood for the doctrine of loose construction. In his first public address after his inauguration,[1] he said:

"We hear much in these days of the usurpation or extension of power by the executive branch. As long as the legislative branch has the power of the purse, the danger of executive usurpation is imaginative. The real danger arises from the disposition of the legislative branch to assume that it has the omnipotence of parliament and may completely control the discretion conferred upon the Executive by the Constitution."

While the doctrine of loose construction has often been affirmed by the courts, the justification has resulted from a very limited number of provisions under Section VIII. of the Constitution, in which certain very definite powers have been granted to Congress. The exercise of those powers granted in paragraphs 1, 2, 3, and 18 of Section VIII. has most often called into question the limitation of Congressional power, both in the

[1] See memorial address on Grover Cleveland, delivered in New York on March 18, 1909.

courts and in political debate. The first paragraph gives to Congress power "to pay the debts and provide for the common defense and general welfare of the United States"; the second, "to borrow money on the credit of the United States," and the third, "to regulate commerce with foreign Nations, and among the several States, and with the Indian tribes." This is true especially of that phrase, "among the several states," in the third paragraph, and the eighteenth, which is the general clause which gives to Congress power "to make all laws which shall be necessary and proper for carrying into execution the foregoing powers, etc." The commerce clause (paragraph 3) has been more often referred to by the courts than any other clause of the Constitution, and since the passage of the Interstate Commerce Act, under the power implied in this clause, in 1884, and the recognition of the constitutionality of the act by the courts, it is becoming more and more important.

Growing out of the financial plans of Alexander Hamilton, Congress, in 1791, passed the law creating the first United States bank. In defending his scheme Hamilton first announced the doctrine of loose construction and implied powers, and became its chief defender. The power to "emit bills of credit and make them legal tender in payment of debts" was denied to the Federal Government by the Constitution. The Constitutional Convention, by a vote of nine states to two, refused to confer this power upon the Federal

Government. So the friends of the bank sought justification in the power granted to Congress "to borrow money upon the credit of the United States." The constitutionality of the Bank Act was upheld in the historic opinion of Marshall in the case of M'Cullough *v.* The State of Maryland.[1] This is the language used:

"Among the enumerated powers, we do not find that of establishing a bank or creating a corporation. But there is no phrase in the instrument which, like the Articles of Confederation, excludes incidental or implied powers, and which requires that everything granted shall be expressly and minutely described. A constitution, to contain an accurate detail of all the subdivisions of which its great powers will admit, and of all the means by which they may be carried into execution, would partake of the prolixity of a legal code, and could scarcely be embraced by the human mind. It would probably never be understood by the public. Its nature, therefore, requires that only its great outlines should be marked, its important objects designated, and the minor ingredients which compose those objects be deduced from the nature of the objects themselves."

The opinion was concluded with the following important generalization:

"Let the end be legitimate, let it be within the scope of the Constitution, and all means which are appropriate, which are plainly adapted to that

[1] 4 Wheaton, 316.

end, which are not prohibited, but consistent with the letter and spirit of the Constitution, are constitutional."

The first Federal decision involving the commerce clause was that of Gibbons *v.* Ogden.[1] All the early litigation growing out of this clause was due to the attempt of the states to enforce legislative enactments which were restricted to the Federal Government under the authority of this paragraph. The most important of these state decisions was that of Livingston and Fulton *v.* Van Ingen, a New York case and reported in 9 Johns, 507. Congress did not attempt to legislate under the power of this clause until within recent times. Since 1884, the courts have been busy upholding the power of Congress in the exercise of its powers under this paragraph. In the case referred to, a New York statute was declared inoperative and void that attempted to give to Livingston and Fulton the exclusive carrying trade on the waters within the state. In Gibbons *v.* Ogden, Chief Justice Marshall again reasserted the doctrine of loose construction, justifying it in this case upon the authority of the "elastic clause."[2] He said:

" This instrument contains an enumeration of powers expressly granted by the people to their government. It has been said that these powers ought to be strictly construed. But why ought

[1] 9 Wheaton, 1.　　　　[2] Section VIII., clause 18.

they to be so construed? Is there one sentence in the Constitution which gives countenance to this rule? In the last of the enumerated powers—that which grants, expressly, the means for carrying all others into execution—Congress is authorized to make all laws which shall be necessary and proper for the purpose. But this limitation on the means which may be used is not extended to the powers which are conferred; nor is there one sentence in the Constitution which has been pointed out by the gentlemen of the bar, or which we have been able to discern, that prescribes this rule. We do not, therefore, think ourselves justified in adopting it. What do the gentlemen mean by a strict construction? If they contend only against that enlarged construction, which would extend words beyond their natural and obvious import, we might question the application of the term, but we should not controvert the principle. If they contend for that narrow construction which, in support of some theory not to be found in the Constitution, would deny to the Government those powers which the words of the grant, as usually understood, import, and which are consistent with the general views and objects of the instrument; for that narrow construction, which would cripple the Government, and render it unequal to the objects for which it is declared to be instituted, to which the powers given, as fairly understood, render it competent; we cannot perceive the propriety of this strict construction, nor adopt it as the rule by which the Constitution is to be expounded. We know of no rule for construing the extent of such powers, other than is given by the language of the instrument which confers them, taken in connection with the purposes for which they were conferred."

The effect of this decision was to establish the doctrine in unmistakable terms, as far as judicial power could establish any governmental principle. We find, however, that the Supreme Court attempted to restrict the principle to those clauses referred to in a preceding paragraph. For instance, in the case of Pennsylvania v. The Wheeling and Belmont Bridge Company,[1] we find that the Court refused to apply the doctrine to the power granted to Congress "to establish post-roads." The Court used this language:

" We do not enter upon the question, whether or not Congress possess the power, under the authority in the Constitution 'to establish post-roads,' to legalize this bridge; for, conceding no such powers can be derived from this clause, it must be admitted that it is, at least, necessarily included in the power conferred to regulate commerce among the several States."

The commerce clause under this construction has had the effect of greatly multiplying the Congressional enactments under its provision.

" Before the year 1840 the construction of this clause had been involved in but five cases submitted to the Supreme Court of the United States. In 1860 the number of cases in that Court involving its construction had increased to twenty; in 1870 the number was thirty; by 1880 the number had increased to seventy-seven; in 1890 it was one hun-

[1] 18 Howard, 421.

dred and forty-eight; while at the present time it is over two hundred."[1]

The Supreme Court met with its greatest difficulty in applying the doctrine of loose construction to the second clause of Section VIII., which gave Congress power "to borrow money on the credit of the United States," due largely to the widely different conditions under which this power was invoked. The Court met with no difficulty in applying the doctrine in the case of the Bank of Commerce *v.* New York City,[2] in which this power was cited in support of the principle that Congress had the right to pass a law exempting stock of the United States from state taxation. But a greater difficulty was encountered when the Court came to apply this clause in justification of legal tender. Upon this question the Supreme Court decided in three different ways, an unprecedented fact in the history of the Court. The first case involving the constitutionality of the Legal Tender acts was that of Hepburn *v.* Griswold,[3] in which the Court held the act unconstitutional. A little later, the Court held the Legal Tender acts constitutional on the ground of public necessity and expediency for self-preservation as a result of the Civil War. The Court finally, in the case of Julliard *v.* Greenbaum,[4] came straight out and held these acts constitutional on the

[1] Putney's *Constitutional Law*, p. 385.　　[2] 2 Black, 620.
[3] 8 Wallace, 603.　　　　　　　　　　[4] 110 U. S., 421.

broad grounds of the power of Congress not only to provide for the common defense, but also as a result of the power "to borrow money on the credit of the United States." This decision was rendered in 1884, and doubtless carries the doctrine of loose construction further than any other opinion ever announced by the Supreme Court.

It is clear from these decisions that in spite of political opposition the principle is an established one in the courts of the country. It is important to observe that the doctrine grows out of a very limited number of the enumerated powers granted to Congress. It might be fairly asked, to what extent can the doctrine be carried in applying the powers of Congress to legislative enactment? A limit must be fixed to the extent of the doctrine, otherwise the Constitution will cease to be any safeguard whatever. Pomeroy, in his *Constitutional Law*,[1] has answered the question in conformity to the views of Chief Justice Marshall, as follows:

"If a particular measure has such a connection or relation with one or more of the enumerated powers granted to Congress or to the Government that it can be seen in any degree or under any state of circumstances to promote the efficiency of such power—or, in other words, that such power can be seen to be made in any degree or under any circumstances operative through its instrumentality—then the measure is within the competency

[1] Bennett's Edition, p. 223.

of Congress to enact; that body alone is the judge
of the closeness of the relation or the extent and
degree of the efficiency, and having judged, the
courts cannot review its decision.   The same
doctrine may be expressed in another form: It is
not within the province of the courts, in the
exercise of their function of examining into the
validity of statutes, to pass upon a question,
which, when reduced to its lowest terms, is one
purely of political economy."

Possibly this is the best and clearest statement
that has been made as to the extent to which the
doctrine can be carried.

Although the doctrine has a permanent place in
our political system, still, with every new application, it will be contested by some political party.
The Democratic party has most consistently taught
the doctrine of strict construction and the Republican party the doctrine of loose construction.

"In general, the views on the interpretation of
the Constitution held by Hamilton and the Federalists have been those of the Whig and the Republican parties, and those held by Jefferson and the
Anti-Federalists have constituted the guiding principles of the Democratic party.   Strictly speaking,
however, the party in power have been loose constructionists and their opponents have been strict
constructionists."[1]

The view here expressed is clearly in accord with
history.   Possibly the greatest value of party

[1] James and Sanford's *Government in State and Nation*, p. 240.

government is in this very fact. Bryce[1] saw the practical necessity for this doctrine when he used the following language:

"The interpretation which has thus stretched the Constitution to cover powers once undreamt of may be deemed a dangerous resource. But it must be remembered that even the constitutions we call rigid must make their choice between being bent or being broken. The Americans have more than once bent their Constitution in order that they might not be forced to break it."

Possibly President Woodrow Wilson sounded the popular note of the present time on this subject when he said "liberal construction of the Federal charter the people want, but not a false construction of it."

[1] *American Commonwealth*, vol. i., p. 390.

CHAPTER III

NATURE OF THE FEDERAL UNION

THE application of the theory of loose construction made possible the centralization of power and the enlargement of the functions of the Federal Government under the Constitution. Out of the question of the relation of the several states to the National Government and the relative power to be exercised by each grew the most fundamental difference between the members of the Federal Convention. The centralizing party and the states' rights party both had able and ardent advocates. This question proved to be an important issue in the various states before the ratification of the Constitution. But with the adoption of the Constitution this ceased to be a question of paramount importance for a time. But it was inevitable that so fundamental a question as that of nationality could not be long evaded or left unsettled. This became increasingly the *vexata quæstio* until the Civil War. The established precedents of the Supreme Court and the application of the principles of the Republican party in the form of legislation made possible the larger definition of nationality in the decade that followed the Civil War. Bryce, writing of this period,[1] says:

"This election [referring to the election of 1876] marks the close of the third period, which embraces the rise and overwhelming predominance of the Republican party. Formed to resist the extension of slavery, led on to destroy it, compelled by circumstances to expand the central authority in a way unthought of before, that party has now worked out its program and fulfilled its original mission. The old aims were accomplished, but new ones had not yet been substituted, for though new problems had appeared, the party was not prepared with solutions. Similarly, the Democratic party had discharged its mission in defending the rights of the reconstructed States, and criticizing excessive executive power; similarly, it too had refused to grapple either with the fresh questions which began to arise since the War, or with the older questions which now reappeared above the subsiding flood of war days. The old parties still stood as organizations, and still claimed to be the exponents of principles. Their respective principles had, however, little direct application to the questions which confronted and divided the country."

The older questions referred to were those of finance and the tariff, neither of which was now to be contested on constitutional grounds; the new questions were those of government of railroads, civil service reform, and the liquor question.

This was a period in which the dominant parties

[1] *American Commonwealth*, Abridged edition, p. 463.

5

were to develop new tendencies. It might be
called the period of political potentiality, the time
for gathering strength with which to grapple with
the problems of the future. Few questions arose
on which one party was to take the affirmative
in the debate and the other party the negative.
Party differences were to be viewed from different angles rather than from diametrically opposite
positions. For instance, the Republican platform
of 1856 was silent on the subject of protection, but
within a few years it was committed to this doctrine; while the Democratic party was favorable
to free trade in its early history, at this period it
has shifted to the mild protection theory, in the
form of a "tariff for revenue only." The present
attitude of these parties may be fairly inferred
from the Republican platform of 1884, and the
Democratic platform of 1892. The political parties
of every shade of belief are in very general accord
at present as to the problems that confront the
country; their differences have grown out of the
nature of the remedy proposed.

But more fundamental and more important than
party attitude with reference to public questions
since the Civil War has been the change in party
sentiment as to the nature of the Federal Union.
The echoes of the Civil War recalled to the attention of the people a basic principle that was, by
incidental inference, to have a marked influence
on the subsequent history of the country. The
Hartford Convention, the doctrine of Nullifica-

tion, and the Secession movement, reveal the fact
that, preceding the Civil War, there was no unity
of conception with reference to the nature of the
Government under which the people lived.   In
the fourth paragraph of the Republican platform
of 1868, we find the word, "Nation," spelled with
a capital letter.   This was the first time the word
had been so used in a platform, and it was not
usually so written in general correspondence before
the War.   The Republican platform also congratu-
lated "the country on the assured success of the
reconstruction policy of Congress."   In answer to
this, the Democratic platform of that year declared "That the Reconstruction acts (so-called),
of Congress, as such, are usurpations and unconstitutional, revolutionary, and void."   The advanced
position that the Republican party took on the
power of the Central Government was the result
of the opposition of the Democratic party to reconstruction, and the prejudice growing out of
the Civil War.   "Nation" was used again in the
Republican platform of 1872, in referring to the
National Government, while the Democratic platforms of this period used the old term, "Federal
Union," in speaking of the Union.

The history of the transformation of the terms
"Federal Government" or. "Confederacy" (as
the General Government was usually referred to
up to the time of the Civil War by both North and
South) into the "Nation" is of interest and consequence in the development of our political ideas.

Lincoln, in his debate with Douglas in 1858, used
the term "Confederacy," in speaking of the
Union, but when Confederacy was applied to the
seceding States in the South, the term was generally abandoned by the North, and with its abandonment the old idea of the word was surrendered
also.   Lincoln, in his Gettysburg address, speaks
of "a new Nation conceived in liberty and dedi-
cated to the proposition that all men are created
equal." From this time on it was often asserted
that we had become a Nation with a big N.   This
is interesting when we contrast this sentiment
with that of the Constitutional Convention; for
in the first draft of the Constitution the word
"national" was struck out twenty-six times and
the words "Government of the United States"
substituted.[1]   But the new word had taken a deep
hold upon the people, and its frequent use by
public speakers and the current literature of the
period gave it permanence in our political vocabu-
lary.   With the appropriation of this term came
the tendency of the party in power to extend the
powers of our governmental agencies, especially
that of the executive power.   Hence, we will find
much in the platforms of the Democratic party
declaring opposition to centralization.   It was but
a step for the Republican party to go from the
Reconstruction acts to a policy of increased centralization; it was but logical for the Democratic

[1] See Thorpe's *Constitutional History of the United States*, vol.
iii., p. 518.

party, in antagonizing the reconstruction policy of the party in power, to oppose, when the time came, the growth of centralization.

The premise for this growth in nationality was carefully laid by the Federal judiciary in the early days of our national existence. As early as February, 1794, Justice Patterson, in rendering an opinion of the Supreme Court,[1] said:

" As to war and peace and their necessary incidents, Congress, by the unanimous voice of the people, exercised exclusive jurisdiction, and stood like Jove, amidst the deities of old, paramount and supreme. The truth is, that the states individually were not known nor recognized as sovereign by foreign nations, nor are they now; the states collectively, under Congress, as the connecting point, or head, were acknowledged by foreign powers, as sovereign, particularly in that acceptation of the term, which is applicable to all great national concerns, and in the exercise of which other sovereigns would be more immediately interested; such for instance, as the rights of war and peace, of making treaties, and sending and receiving ambassadors."

John Marshall, "the right arm of nationality," throughout his brilliant judicial career took this larger view of our national existence. His decision in Cohens v. Virginia[2] which was rendered in 1821, is typical of many that he delivered bearing on the theory of our nationality. Touching this point, he says:

[1] See Penhallow v. Doane, 3 Dallas, 507.
[2] 6 Wheaton, 264.

" That the United States form, for many, and for most important purposes, a single nation, has not yet been denied. In war, we are one people. In making peace, we are one people. In all common regulations, we are one and the same people. In many other respects, the American people are one; and the Government, which is alone capable of controlling and managing their interests, in all these respects is the Government of the Union. It is their Government, and in that character they have no other. America has chosen to be, in many respects, and to many purposes, a nation; and for all these purposes her Government is complete; to all these objects it is competent."

The extent to which the national authority may go was discussed by Marshall in the famous case of United States *v.* Peters.[1] He contended that this power extended to the complete annulment of any State enactment which was decided to be in conflict with the Constitution. His words were significant, yet simple:

" If the legislatures of the several States may at will annul the judgments of the courts of the United States, and destroy the rights acquired under those judgments, the Constitution itself becomes a solemn mockery; and the Nation is deprived of the means of enforcing its laws, by the instrumentality of its own tribunals. So fatal a result must be deprecated by all and the people of Pennsylvania as well as the citizens of every other state must feel a deep interest in resisting principles so destructive of

[1] 3 Dallas, p. 121.

the Union, and in averting consequences so fatal to themselves."

One year later, in 1810, Marshall reënforced this decision with that of Fletcher *v.* Peck.[1] Here again the dignity and authority of the nation were unmistakably declared:

"But Georgia cannot be viewed as a single, unconnected, sovereign power, on whose legislature no other restrictions are imposed than may be found in its own constitution. She is a part of a large empire; she is a member of the American Union; and that Union has a Constitution the supremacy of which all acknowledge, and which imposes limits to the legislatures of the several states, which none claim a right to pass."

These are typical of the opinions of Marshall on the theory of nationality. There are too many of his decisions that bear upon this point to quote or refer to them all. During the thirty-four years that Marshall was upon the Supreme Bench he delivered the opinion in five hundred and nineteen cases. Sixty-two of these cases involved questions of constitutional law; of this number, Marshall himself wrote thirty-six. During the period that he sat upon the Supreme Bench, there was more unanimity of opinion and fewer "majority decrees" than has ever existed since his day. "Very rarely was there given a dissenting opinion, and only once was the Chief Justice compelled to give

[1] 6 Cranch, p. 87.

a dissenting opinion from that of the majority of the Court. It is nearer correct to say that in all except one case the majority of the Court joined the great Chief Justice in his opinion." This fact is important when we consider his influence and legal learning, which inspired the people generally with confidence in his decisions, in connection with his views of the nature of our Federal Union. He saw with great discernment the two opposing views of the followers of Hamilton and Jefferson, for he said:

" The whole country was divided between two great political parties; the one of which contemplated America as a nation and labored incessantly to invest the Federal head with powers competent to the preservation of the Union, and the other, attached to the state governments, viewed all the powers of Congress with jealousy and assented reluctantly to measures which would enable the head to act in any respect independently of the members."

It is clear from this quotation to which party he gave his sympathy, and he did more than give his sympathy, he gave his theory the dignity of law by writing his opinions consistent with his views.

The opinions, quotations from which are taken above, are typical of the judicial mind on the subject of nationality before the Civil War. It is interesting to observe the caution the courts used in referring to the supreme power of the National Government. Even Marshall speaks of the Federal

Union as a "single nation, for many, and for most important purposes," and, in the main, leaves this generalization as a precedent for future application. The fact is, our nationality has been a growth, the extent of which had not been defined in the Constitution. Viewed in the light of political science, we had always been a nation; the question was to what extent we had become a state. There is both an etymological and historical distinction between nation and state. Nation is derived from *natio* (from *nasci*) and indicates birth and race, *populus* and *polis* both refer to the political life exercised by the nation (*natio*). Historically, the nation precedes the state. The national spirit (*volksgeist*) precedes the national will (*volkswille*). The period of this precedence may be long or short, depending on many conditions both of an internal and external nature. In Germany the national spirit preceded by many centuries the national will, while in America the period was comparatively brief. It is always the natural tendency of a nation to seek expression in the state. This fact has caused Bluntschli[1] to say, "The idea of a nation always bears a necessary relation to the state, and we may say, No nation, no state." He modifies this by saying that "a despot knows nothing of nations, only of subjects." If we merge a collective personality (the nation) into a national will (the state), we obtain what society usually designates by the

[1] *The Theory of the State*, p. 86.

single term, nation. "By a nation (*volk*) we generally understand a society of all the members of a state as united and organized in the state." It is evident that state and nation were regarded as synonymous terms by the judiciary, the word nation being preferred to state, as the latter was the nomenclature of the largest subdivision of the nation. It was in this sense that "Nation" was used in the party platforms, especially that of the Republican party.

The question that grew out of the political agitation of the time, was in what sense the word "state" was used in the Constitution. The literature of political science is rich in definitions of the term. Professor Holland[1] says, "A state is a numerous assemblage of human beings, generally occupying a certain territory, amongst whom the will of the majority or of an ascertainable class of persons is, by the strength of such a majority or class, made to prevail against any of their number who oppose it." "A state," says Woodrow Wilson,[2] "is a people organized for law within a definite territory." Wolsey[3] gives this definition: "The body or community which thus by permanent law, through its organs, administers justice within certain limits of territory is called a state." Do either or all of these definitions apply to the meaning or meanings of the term "state" as used in our Federal Constitution? This

[1] *Elements of Jurisprudence.*
[2] *The State.*   [3] *Political Science.*

question was carefully considered in the short, but important, decision of Texas *v.* White.[1] In no other judicial opinion, nor perhaps in the literature of political science, can there be found so learned a discussion of the meaning of this term as used in our Constitution, as in the illuminating opinion of Chief Justice Chase in this case.

With reference to the looseness with which the term has been used, the Court said:

"State describes sometimes a people or community of individuals united more or less closely in political relations, inhabiting temporarily or permanently the same country; often it denotes only the country or territory, inhabited by such a community; not infrequently it is applied to the government under which the people live; at other times it represents the combined idea of people, territory, and government. This is undoubtedly the fundamental idea upon which the republican institutions of our own country are established."

For this last assertion the Court cites Penhallow *v.* Doane, 3 Dallas, page 93.

The Court then proceeds to show that the term has been used in our Constitution in three distinct senses, as follows:

(1) In the Constitution the term "state" most frequently expresses the combined idea just noticed of people, territory, and government. A state, in the ordinary sense of the Constitution, is a political community of free citizens, occupying a

[1] 7 Wallace, 700.

territory of defined boundaries, and organized
under a government sanctioned and limited by a
written constitution, and established by the consent of the governed.   It is the union of such states
under a common constitution which forms the
distinct and greater political unit, which that
Constitution designates as the United States, and
makes the people and states which compose it one
people and one country.

(2) It is also used in its geographical sense, as
in the clauses which require that a representative
in Congress shall be an inhabitant of the state in
which he shall be chosen, and that the trial of
crimes shall be held within the state where
committed.

(3) "And there are instances where the principal sense of the word seems to be that primary
one to which we have adverted, of a people or
political community, as distinguished from a government, as in the clause that guarantees to every
State in the Union a republican form of government.   In this clause a plain distinction is made
between a state and the government of a state."

The nature and growth of the nation into the
state is described as follows:

"The union of the States was never a purely
artificial and arbitrary relation.   It began among
the Colonies, and grew out of common origin,
mutual sympathies, kindred principles, similar interests, and geographical relations.   It was con-
firmed and strengthened by the necessities of war,

and received definite form and character, and sanction from the Articles of Confederation. By these the Union was solemnly declared 'to be perpetual.' And when these Articles were found to be inadequate to the exigencies of the country, the Constitution was ordained 'to form a more perfect Union.' It is difficult to convey the idea of indissoluble unity more clearly than by these words. What can be indissoluble if a perpetual Union, made more perfect, is not? The Constitution, in all its provisions, looks to an *indestructible Union, composed of indestructible States.* When, therefore Texas became one of the United States, she entered into an indissoluble relation. All the obligations of perpetual Union, and all the guarantees of republican government in the Union, attached at once to the State. The union between Texas and the other States was as complete, as perpetual, and as indissoluble as the union between the original States. There was no place for reconsideration, or revocation, except through revolution, or through consent of the States."

The effect of this decision is to give to the Federal Government the supreme right to the title of "The State." "The separate 'States' of the American Union are not states in the technical sense of the term, since each forms part of the single entirety known as the United States. The United States as a totality constitutes a state; the 'State' of Massachusetts does not."[1]

The nature and strength of the National Union was discussed from a different view-point by Jus-

[1] Leacock's *Elements of Political Science*, p. 14.

tice Swayne in delivering the opinion in the case of White *v.* Hart and Davis. [1]

"The National Constitution was, as the preamble recites, ordained and established by the people of the United States. It created not a confederacy of States, but a government of individuals. It assumed that the Government and the Union, which it created, and the States which were incorporated into the Union, would be indestructible and perpetual; and as far as human means could accomplish such a work, it intended to make them so. The government of the Nation and the government of the States are each alike absolute and independent of each other in their respective spheres of action; but the former is as much a part of the Government of the people of each State, and is as much entitled to their allegiance and obedience as their own State governments—'the Constitution of the United States and the laws made in pursuance thereof' being in all cases when they apply the supreme law of the land. For all the purposes of the National Government, the people of the United States are a composite mass, and their unity and identity, in this view of the subject, are not affected by their segregation by State lines for the purposes of State government and local administration. Considered in this connection, the States are organisms for the performance of their appropriate functions in the vital system of the larger policy, of which, in this aspect of the subject, they form a part, and which would perish if they were all stricken from existence or ceased to perform their allotted work."

[1] 13 Wallace, 646.

In conformity to this decision the Republican platform of 1880 in its second plank declared that

"The Constitution of the United States is a supreme law of the land and not a mere contract. Out of confederated States it made a sovereign Nation. Some powers are denied to the Nation, while others are denied to the States; but the boundary between the powers delegated and those reserved is to be determined by the National, and not by the State tribunals. "

Based on the views contained in the decisions cited above, we find the first platform demands on the subject of the regulation of interstate commerce in the platforms of 1884. Both of the leading parties saw a solution to the problem of the evils growing out of monopolistic corporations in the extended powers bestowed or recognized in the National Government. The Democratic platform of 1884, upon which Cleveland was nominated and elected President, declared the party favorable to legislation that would lead "to the prevention of monopoly and the strict enforcement of individual rights against corporate abuses." The Republican platform of the same year contained the following unequivocal declarations: "We recognize the regulation of commerce with foreign nations and between the States as one of the most important prerogatives of the General Government," and that "the principle of public regulation of railway corporations is a salutary one for the protection of all the people; and we favor legislation that shall prevent unjust discriminations and excessive charges for transportation."

While the courts had recognized the right of Congress to legislate concerning waterways[1] from a very early date, it seems that the power of Congress over land transportation had been somewhat in doubt. But the newer meaning given to the Constitution, and the doctrine of loose construction which had long been recognized, made it possible for Federal legislation to remedy the abuse of power by private corporations, which had grown in wealth and influence since the time when the states first began to pass general incorporation acts in 1850.

The attitude of the Supreme Court on the question was further evidenced by their decision in the case of Robbins v. Shelby County Taxing District,[2] which held that we were but one country, and must be subject to one system of regulations, and not to a multitude of such systems, with reference to interstate commerce. This decision was rendered in 1886, and shortly thereafter, the Court handed down its decision in the Wabash case,[3] which denied to a state the power to control or regulate interstate shipments.

So on February 4, 1887, Congress passed "the Cullom Act," otherwise known as "the Interstate Commerce Act," for the regulation of interstate

[1] See Gibbons v. Ogden, 9 Wheaton, 1.
[2] 120 U.S., 489.   [3] 118 U. S., 564.

railway traffic. As was to be expected from previous decisions, no serious questions arose as to the constitutionality of the act. The Supreme Court defined its attitude with reference to the act in the Import Rate case.[1]

" As the powers of States were restricted to their own territories and did not enable them efficiently to control the management of great corporations whose roads extend throughout the entire country, there was a general demand that Congress, in the exercise of plenary power over the subject of foreign and interstate commerce, should deal with the evils complained of by a general enactment, and the statute in question was the result."

The constitutionality of the Interstate Commerce Act, for the regulation of interstate railways, led Congress to infer the right to regulate any corporation or trust engaged in interstate commerce. So in 1890, Congress passed the Sherman Anti-Trust Act, which penalized all illegal acts of corporations, the illegal acts being defined in the act itself. This act was questioned on the ground that it violated the freedom of contract guaranteed by the Fifth Amendment to the Constitution of the United States. But the Supreme Court in many decisions has upheld the constitutionality of this act also.[2]

[1] 162 *United States*, 211.

[2] See U. S. *v.* Joint Traffic Association, 171 United States, 505; Addyson Pipe and Steel Company *v.* U. S., 175 U. S., 211; and *Judson on Interstate Commerce.*

6

It is impossible to correctly estimate or define the growth of centralization in our National Government in recent times. Since the Civil War, the three departments of Government have worked hand in hand in this extension. We are far away from the conception the Fathers had of the powers of the Federal Union in 1800, and nothing gives evidence of this fact more conclusively than the effects of the Federal laws governing corporate wealth. The full effect of these laws has not yet been realized by the people; either in their own application or in their influence on the future legislation of the country. Whether these future laws will prove helpful or detrimental, will depend on the clearness with which our lawmakers see the necessity of providing for national development without destroying the identity of our organic structure. On this point Bluntschli has offered a principle of guidance of great value:

"A nation outlives the changing phases of its development, and although it remains essentially the same, yet its needs and views alter with the periods of its life. A national and popular state adapts its organism to the continual development of the nation, but without completely losing its identity."

CHAPTER IV

IMPERIALISM *v.* EXPANSION

PREVIOUS to the issue that grew out of the annexation of Hawaii, the American people accepted with great equanimity the Gladstone doctrine "that the sea was a divider and not a uniter of nations." The issue was late in developing in this country because of the large area that remained unoccupied in the West. Not until we had extended our power as a nation to the shore line of the Pacific and had begun to look out over the Pacific did expansion develop into imperialism. The same influence that carried the trapper and adventurer to the West in an early day, carried this same class to the Hawaiian Islands when the West was settled. The native was taught the blessings of commerce by these traders, the blessings of Christianity were soon carried by the missionary, and these two forces made logical and easy the hoisting of the American flag. These were the steps by which we first set the precedent upon which to build an imperialistic government.

Expansion was a problem before imperialism was thought of. By what authority, and in what manner, we were to govern territory purchased

since the adoption of the Constitution, has been a
serious and important problem in our governmental history. The question first arose when
Louisiana was purchased from France. As has
been previously shown, President Jefferson seriously doubted executive or legislative power to acquire by purchase any territory for the purpose of
making it a part of the United States. So firmly
was he convinced of this fact, that, when negotiations were under way for this territory, he
instructed Livingston not to assert that this territory was to be incorporated as a part of the United
States, for he thought such a provision would be
illegal. Through the insistence of Bonaparte,
Livingston disobeyed instructions and approved
the third section of the treaty which reads as
follows: "That the inhabitants of the ceded territory shall be incorporated into the Union of the
United States, and admitted as soon as possible,
according to the principles of the Federal Constitution, to the enjoyment of all the rights, advantages, and immunities of citizens of the United
States."

Jefferson's views on the subject were clearly
presented in a letter to Senator Breckenridge of
Kentucky, dated August 12, 1803. He said:

"This treaty must, of course, be laid before both
Houses, because both have important functions to
exercise respecting it. They, I presume, will see
their duty to their country in ratifying and paying for it, so as to secure a good which would

otherwise probably be never again in their power. But I suppose they must then appeal to the Nation for an additional article to the Constitution approving and confirming an act which the Nation had not previously authorized. The Constitution has made no provision for holding foreign territory, still less for incorporating foreign nations into our Union."

Jefferson himself prepared two amendments to the Constitution, the first of which declared "The province of Louisiana is incorporated with the United States and made a part thereof," and the second defining, in general terms, the rights of the citizens of the territory. But for some reason this matter was never pressed, and these amendments were never submitted to the people for ratification.[1]

When bills were introduced into Congress to provide the purchase money, and also a civil government for this territory, the constitutionality of incorporating Louisiana into the Union was vigorously debated. But the administration forces won on the ground that under the treaty-making power Congress could acquire territory and hold it under the laws of Congress and the Constitution. This question was not adjudicated by the courts at this time.

In 1819, Florida was purchased from Spain. Three years later Congress passed a series of acts for the government of the territory. The relation

[1] *Jefferson's Writings*, vol. viii., p. 269.

of this territory to the states and the Constitution was discussed by the Supreme Court in American Insurance Company *v.* 356 Bales of Cotton.[1] Mr. Justice Johnson, of the Supreme Court, presided over the Circuit Court, and delivered this opinion. He said:

"It becomes indispensable to the solution of these difficulties that we should conceive a just idea of the relation in which Florida stands to the United States. The question now to be considered relates to territories previously subject to the acknowledged jurisdiction of another sovereignty, such as was Florida to the Crown of Spain. And on this subject we have the most explicit proof that the understanding of our public functionaries is that the Government and laws of the United States do not extend to such territory by the mere act of cession."

On appeal from the decision of the Circuit Court to the Supreme Court, Marshall held that Florida upon the ratification of the treaty became a territory of the United States and subject to the power of Congress under the territorial clause.[2]

In Dred Scott *v.* Sanford[3] the Court carefully considered the power of Congress under the Constitution to acquire territory outside of the original limits of the United States, and what powers might be exercised therein over persons and property. The Court used this language:

[1] 1 Peters, 511.   [2] Constitution, Art. IV., Sec. III., par. 2.
[3] 19 Howard, 393.

"There is certainly no power given by the Constitution to the Federal Government to establish or maintain colonies bordering on the United States or at a distance, to be ruled and governed at its own pleasure; and if a new State is admitted, it needs no further legislation by Congress, because the Constitution itself defines the relative rights and powers and duties of the State, and the citizens of the State, and the Federal Government. But no power is given to acquire territory to be held and governed permanently in that character."

The territorial clause of the Federal Constitution was cited by the Supreme Court eight times before the date of the acquisition of our first insular territory. The general rule might be deduced from all these opinions to the effect that

"Congress has absolute power to govern the territories of the United States, whether that power is incident to its capacity to acquire territory as a sovereign, or whether it is derived from the provisions of this clause which gives to Congress power to dispose of and make all needful rules and regulations respecting the territory or other property belonging to the United States."[1]

As to the power to acquire territory, the Supreme Court has taken the following position: "The Constitution confers absolutely upon the Government of the Union the powers of making war and of making treaties; consequently, that

[1] See Boutwell's *The Constitution of the United States at the end of the First Century*, chapter xliii.

Government possesses the power of acquiring territory either by conquest or by treaty."[1]   This doctrine was also proclaimed in the Dred Scott case, the Court taking the view, however, that, while territory could be legally acquired, it must be acquired for the purpose of finally admitting the territory into the Union as states, and not with the view of holding it permanently as a colonial possession, as has been shown above. Pomeroy says[2]:

"Indeed, none but those who would interpret the Constitution as though it were a penal statute have ever doubted the authority of the Nation, through some one of its governmental agents, to acquire new territory and add it to the domain of the United States.   Congress may declare war, and the President, as commander-in-chief, may wage war.   One of the most common results of war is conquest; and unless the wars of this country are to be carried on differently from those of other nations, and unless we are to be deprived of the advantages of success, the possibility of conquest must be considered as included within the capacity to declare and wage war.   The President, with the advice and consent of two thirds of the Senate, may make treaties.   No kinds of treaties are specified; no limitations are placed; the language is as broad as possible; indeed, these international compacts are expressly declared to be the supreme law of the land.   No species of treaty is more common than that of cession; and unless

[1] American Insurance Co. v. Canter, 1 Peters, 511.
[2] Constitutional Law, p. 397, Bennett's Edition.

we would interpolate a restriction which the language of the Constitution does not require, and thereby place the United States in a condition of inferiority to all other countries, we must admit that territory may be acquired by treaty."

This settled doctrine was somewhat disturbed in 1893, when the question of the annexation of Hawaii began to be agitated. This island had enjoyed favorable commercial rights with us since 1876. When in 1893 a revolution was precipitated which resulted in the dethronement of the Queen, and a republic was established, serious discussion arose with reference to annexation to the United States. While negotiations were under consideration for annexation, an American protectorate was declared, and a commission was appointed to visit the island and investigate conditions. When this commission made its report, President Cleveland, who opposed annexation, dissolved the protectorate and Hawaii was recognized as a republic by the United States.

When the campaign of 1896 came on, the Democrats opposed, while the Republicans favored, the annexation of the islands of Hawaii. The Republican platform declared: "Our foreign policy should be always firm, vigorous, and dignified, and all our interests in the Western Hemisphere carefully watched and guarded. The Hawaiian Islands should be controlled by the United States, and no foreign power should be permitted to interfere with them." The election of McKinley upon this platform insured the incorporation of Hawaii as a part of the United States. This was effected on July 7, 1898, and two years later the islands were organized as a territory of the United States. President McKinley followed court and judicial precedent in his message to Congress on December 3, 1901, when he said:

"In Hawaii our aim must be to develop the Territory on the traditional American lines. We do not wish a region of large estates tilled by cheap labor; we wish a healthy American community of men who themselves till the farms they own. All our legislation for the islands should be shaped with this end in view."

Three months after the annexation of Hawaii, the Peace Commission appointed by the American and Spanish Governments met in Paris to conclude the terms of peace resulting from the Spanish-American War. As a result of their deliberations, (1) Spain recognized the freedom of Cuba; (2) Porto Rico and Guam were ceded to the United States; and (3) for a consideration of $20,000,000, the Philippines were acquired by the United States. When the question of ratifying this treaty came up in the Senate, the most violent opposition grew out of the purchase of the Philippine Islands. It was believed that instead of proving an aid, these islands would become a real burden to the country. But the treaty was finally ratified without modification, and we took the step that carried us from a position of healthy expansion to that of an imperialistic empire.

"Imperialism" was declared by the Democrats in their platform of 1900 to be the "paramount issue."

"We are not opposed [said their platform] to territorial expansion when it takes in desirable territory which can be created into States in the Union, and whose people are willing and fit to become American citizens. We favor expansion by every peaceful and legitimate means. But we are unalterably opposed to the seizing of distant islands to be governed outside the Constitution, and whose people can never become citizens."

The Republican platform made no reference to the subject further than to call attention to the fact that we had acquired the Philippines as a result of the Treaty of Paris. But their platform declared, with reference to the Philippine people, that "The largest measure of self-government consistent with their welfare and our duties shall be secured to them by law."

But the deeper enthusiasm of the Republican party was revealed in the keynote speech of Senator Beveridge in opening the Republican campaign in Chicago on the 25th day of September, 1900. He used this language:

"When an English ship, laden with English goods, bound for the Orient, sails westward, her first sight of land will be Porto Rico—and Cuba, also, as I hope—with the Stars and Stripes above them. As it passes through the wedded waters of the Isthmian Sea, still the Stars and Stripes above them. Half-way across that great American ocean known as the Pacific, the first port of call and exchange will be the Islands of Hawaii, with the Stars and Stripes above them. And farther west, as the land of sunrise and sunset lifts before the eyes of the crew of that merchantman, they will behold glowing in the heavens of the east still again, and still forever, those Stars and Stripes of glory. And if that ship sets sail from Australia for Japan, it must stop and trade in ports of the greatest commercial stronghold in the world, the Philippine Islands, with the Stars and Stripes above each one of them."

The effect of this speech was to commit formally the Republican party to the doctrine of imperialism, and to attract the attention of the whole country to this as an issue.

The speech of Senator Beveridge was in perfect harmony with the platform of the Republican party in that year. A strong plank was incorporated on the policy of the party with reference to the territory acquired through the acceptance of the Treaty of Paris, in which it was asserted that "Our authority could not be less than our responsibility," and that the responsibility before the world was to determine for these in our new possessions the measure of self-government they could best use. The Democratic platform was still more emphatic in declaring opposition to the doctrine. It was declared that "The Constitution

follows the Flag," and the platform further denounced the doctrine that "an Executive or Congress deriving their existence and their powers
from the Constitution can exercise lawful authority beyond it or in violation of it." The
platform further declared itself in favor of the acquisition of desirable territory, but unalterably
opposed to imperialism, and declared this to be
the paramount issue. A sentence in the message of
President McKinley sent to Congress on December 5, 1899, which asserted that "As long as the
insurrection [in the Philippines] continues, the
military arm of the Government must necessarily
be supreme," furnished the material out of which
the Democrats made a definition of imperialism.
"Imperialism," they said, "is the policy of governing colonial possessions by force in contrast to
a policy of expansion granting full self-government
to such colonies."

These conflicting doctrines were subject to a
speedy review by the highest Court in the land
soon after the inauguration in 1901. In the latter
days of May of that year the Supreme Court
handed down its decision in the famous Insular
Tariff cases.[1] Justice Brown rendered the opinion
in all these cases. Each opinion was rendered by
a bare majority (5 to 4), Chief Justice Fuller
being among the dissenting judges. The Court

---

[1] See De Lima *v.* Bidwell, 182 U. S., 1; Goetz *v.* U. S., 182
U. S., 219; Dooley *v.* U. S., 182 U. S., 222; Armstrong *v.* U. S.,
182 U. S., 243; and Downs *v.* U. S., 182 U. S., 246.

decided in substance that the Constitution does not necessarily follow the flag, and that Congress has full power to deal with our recently acquired territory as it sees fit.

The insular cases were largely influenced by three important cases which were also the result of litigation over tariff duties,—The United States v. Rice,[1] Fleming v. Page,[2] and Cross v. Harrison.[3]

In The United States v. Rice it was held that military occupation of any territory, even if for a temporary period, gave the fullest right of sovereignty to the country then in possession, even if the territory was surrendered later.

The case of Fleming v. Page was somewhat to the converse of this. This was an action brought to recover duties collected on goods imported from Tampico, Mexico, when this place was in temporary occupation by the soldiers of the United States. It was held that this town was still foreign territory even when occupied by our soldiers. Chief Justice Taney observed:

"The United States, it is true, may extend its boundaries by conquest, or treaty, and may demand the cession of territory as the condition of peace, in order to indemnify its citizens for the injuries they have suffered, or reimburse the Government for the expenses of the war. But this can only be done by the treaty-making power conferred upon the President by the declaration of war. While it was occupied by our troops they

[1] 4 Wheaton, 246.   [2] 9 Howard, 603.   [3] 16 Howard, 164.

were in an enemy's country, and not in their own; the inhabitants were still foreigners and enemies and owed to the United States nothing more than a submission and obedience sometimes called temporary allegiance, which is due from a conquered enemy, when he surrenders to a force which he is unable to resist."

The third case was that of Cross *v.* Harrison. This was an action of assumpsit to recover money that had been paid Harrison while acting as collector for goods imported into California from foreign countries between the second day of February, 1848, the date of the treaty of peace between the United States and Mexico, and November 13, 1849, when the collector was appointed by the President under an express law of Congress. It was insisted by the plaintiff that California was not foreign territory after the date of the ratification of the treaty. The opinion in this case established three propositions:

"1. That under the war power the military governor of California was authorized to prescribe a scale of duties upon importations from foreign countries to San Francisco, and to collect the same through a collector appointed by himself, until the ratification of the treaty of peace.

"2. That after such ratification, duties were legally exacted under the tariff laws of the United States, which took effect immediately.

"3. That the civil government established in California continued from the necessities of the case until Congress provided a territorial government."

It will be seen that the three propositions involve the recognition of the fact that California became domestic territory immediately upon the ratification of the treaty, or, to speak more accurately, as soon as this was officially known in California. The doctrine that a port ceded to, and occupied by us, does not lose its foreign character until Congress has acted, and a collector is appointed, was distinctly repudiated with the apparent acquiescence of Chief Justice Taney, who wrote the opinion in Fleming v. Page.

This was the status of the question when the insular cases came up for trial. In De Lima v. Bidwell the suit was the result of an attempt to recover money paid as duty on sugar shipped from Porto Rico. The only question was whether Porto Rico was a foreign country at the time the sugar was shipped. The tariff act, under review, provided that "there shall be levied, collected, and paid upon all articles imported from foreign countries, duties," etc.

The Court began by citing the cases of United States v. Rice, Fleming v. Page, and Cross v. Harrison from which the following conclusion was drawn:

"It is evident that, from 1803, the date of Mr. Gallatin's letter, to the present time, there is not a shred of authority except the dictum in Fleming v. Page (practically overruled in Cross v. Harrison) for holding that a district ceded to and in the possession of the United States remains for any purpose a foreign country. Both of these conditions must exist to produce a change of nationality for revenue purposes. Possession is not alone sufficient, as was held in Fleming *v.* Page; nor is a treaty ceding such territory sufficient without a surrender of possession. Keens *v.* McDonough, 8 Peters, 308; Pollard's Heirs *v.* Kibbe, 14 Peters, 353, 406; Hallett *v.* Hunt, 7 Ala., 882, 899; The Anna, 5 Rob., 97. The practice of the executive departments thus continued for more than half a century, is entitled to great weight, and should not be disregarded nor overturned except for cogent reasons, and unless it be clear that such construction be erroneous. U. S. *v.* Johnston, 124 U. S., 236, and other cases cited."

The Court then proceeds to show that foreign territory could be both ceded and acquired through the power given to Congress and the Executive to make treaties, and acquired "as absolutely as if the annexation were made, as in the case of Texas and Hawaii, by an act of Congress. So by the ratification of the Treaty of Paris the island became territory of the United States, although not an organized territory in the technical sense of the word."

Can a country become domestic territory for one purpose and foreign for another? The Court answers in the negative.

" The theory that a country remains foreign with respect to the tariff laws until Congress has acted by embracing it within the customs union, presupposes that a country may be domestic for one purpose and foreign for another. It may un-

7

doubtedly become necessary for the adequate administration of a domestic territory to pass a special act providing the proper machinery and officers, as the President would have no authority, except under the war power, to administer it himself, but no act is necessary to make a domestic territory if once it had been ceded to the United States. We express no opinion as to whether Congress is bound to appropriate money to pay for it. This has been much discussed by writers upon Constitutional law, but it is not necessary to consider it in this case, as Congress made prompt appropriation of the money stipulated in the treaty. This theory also presupposes that territory may be held indefinitely by the United States; that it may be treated in every particular, except for tariff purposes, as domestic territory; that laws may be enacted and enforced by officers of the United States sent there for that purpose; that insurrection may be suppressed, wars carried on, revenues collected, taxes imposed,—in short, everything can be done which a government can do, within its own boundaries,—and yet that territory may still remain a foreign country. That this state of things may continue for years, for a century even, but that it still remains a foreign country. To hold that this can be done as a matter of law we deem to be pure judicial legislation.

"We are therefore of the opinion that at the time these duties were levied Porto Rico was not a foreign country within the meaning of the tariff laws but a territory of the United States, that the duties were illegally exacted, and that the plaintiffs are entitled to recover them back."

Mr. Justice McKenna filed a dissenting opinion in this case, in which Justices Shiras and White concurred. He declared that Porto Rico "occupied a relation to the United States between that of being a foreign country absolutely and of being a domestic territory absolutely." "This view," said Justice McKenna, "vindicates the Government from national and international weaknesses. It exhibits the Constitution as a charter of great and vital authorities, with limitations indeed, but with such limitations as serve and assist government, not destroy it."   In Goetz *v.* United States[1] and Grossman *v.* United States[2] the same question was in issue as that in De Lima *v.* Bidwell, and was similarly decided.

In the cases of Dooley *v.* United States and Armstrong *v.* United States[3] the converse of the preceding cases was involved. The question was, had Congress the right to lay duties on goods shipped into Porto Rico. The question turned on the meaning of the "United States" as used in our Constitution. Did the term include the territories and colonies subsequently acquired by the United States? In the case of Dooley *v.* United States, the majority of the Court held that our tariff laws began to operate on import duty in Porto Rico when the treaty of peace was ratified, and reciprocally from the same date the right to collect import duties from the United States into that island ceased.

The same question was decided with reference to the Philippines in the case of Fourteen Diamond

[1] 182 U. S., 221.   [2] 182 U. S., 222.   [3] 182 U. S., 243.

Rings v. United States.[1] This case involved the constitutionality of an act laying a duty on goods imported into the United States from the Philippine Islands. The Philippines at that time occupied a somewhat different position, as they do in some respects to-day, from that of the relation of the island of Porto Rico to the United States. This was due to two facts: (1) By the resolution of the United States Senate, adopted by only a majority, and not a two-third majority vote, the Senate stated, "That by the ratification of the treaty of peace with Spain it is not intended to incorporate the inhabitants of the Philippine Islands into citizenship with the United States, nor is it intended to permanently annex said islands as an integral part of the territory of the United States"; and (2) because of the state of insurrection that was being waged by the inhabitants of those islands against the United States at that time. But in spite of the difference in conditions, both legal and martial, the Court followed their decision in De Lima v. Bidwell, and held that the tariff laws applied and were constitutionally in full force and effect.

With this decision, the legal test of our relation to our insular possessions was complete. Imperialism, by this opinion, has become an established doctrine by and through judicial decree.

The political and historical importance of these cases should lead to the thoughtful study of them

[1] 183 U. S., 176.

by every citizen. While it is impossible to give more of the doctrine discussed therein, still the important summary of these cases by Mr. Walter Wellman gives a very accurate idea of the leading points covered.

" 1. The Constitution does not follow the flag *ex propria vigore*—of its own force.

" 2. The United States may enter upon a colonial policy—has already entered upon it—without violation of the Constitution.

" 3. This Nation has all the powers that rightfully belong to a sovereign international state and may acquire territory without incorporating such territory as an integral part of itself.

" 4. The simple act of acquisition by treaty or otherwise does not automatically bring about such incorporation; and incorporation is effected only by the will of the States acting consciously through Congress.

" 5. Porto Rico is not a part of the United States, but 'a territory appurtenant and belonging to the United States.' Tariffs established by Congress upon goods coming from or going to Porto Rico are valid and collectable. The Foraker Act is constitutional.

"6. Congress has full power over the territories, may regulate and dispose of them, may at its discretion extend the Constitution to them, may admit them as States, or may hold them indefinitely as territories, colonies, or dependencies.

"7. Porto Rico is not a 'foreign country,' and therefore the Dingley Law, which levies duties upon goods imported 'from foreign countries,' does not apply to Porto Rico. Nor yet is 'Porto Rico a part of the United States.' It is a domestic territory over which Congress has 'unrestricted control.'"[1]

Putney[2] says with reference to the logic of these cases that:

"In spite of the great differences of opinion as to the law on the question involved in these cases and in spite of the dissenting opinions in these cases, the majority decisions in both of the cases of De Lima v. Bidwell and Downs v. Bidwell, are supported by the unbroken line of decisions of the Supreme Court since the adoption of the Constitution and by the position of the Executive Department on all occasions for the past century. All that stands opposed to these decisions (outside of the dissenting opinions in these cases themselves) is certain dicta in Blake v. Loughborough and Fleming v. Page and the action of the Executive Department in the case of Louisiana."

This statement is, no doubt, true. Nevertheless we find ourselves, as a result of this latter day application of earlier judicial dicta, attempting to control judicially under the Constitution at least five classes of dependencies: (1) Territories, including Hawaii, which have practically as good government as that allowed the neighboring States; (2) Territories under various forms of paternal governments, as, e. g., Alaska and some of the smaller Pacific islands; (3) Territory under the special wardship of the National Government

[1] See W. T. Stead's *The Americanization of the World*, p. 77.
[2] *Constitutional Law*, p. 470.

directly; (4) Territory controlled by a special type of territorial government; and (5) Territory which is subject to special Congressional legislation from time to time, having no settled or fixed outlined policy with reference to its future position, as in the case of the Philippine Islands.

It cannot be questioned that our Constitution did not contemplate such a condition. If we accept the judicial attitude on the subject, we must regard much of this territory as occupying a transitory position with reference to the United States; for clearly we must, in order to be consistent with our organic law, look forward to granting to these dependencies the same degree of self-government as that enjoyed by our organized territory, or else we must bestow upon them complete independence. In no other way can we uphold the fundamental doctrine "that governments derive their just powers from the consent of the governed."

We can agree with Gladstone when he said that "The paramount question of the American future is a vision of territory, population, power, passing beyond all experience. The momentous exhibition to mankind for the first time in history of free institutions on a gigantic scale."

De Tocqueville saw in this same vision the undoing of the American Republic.

"The history of the world affords no instance of a great nation retaining the form of republican government for a long series of years, and this has led to the conclusion that such a state of things is impracticable. For my own part, I cannot but censure the imprudence of attempting to limit the possible and to judge the future on the part of a being who is hourly deceived by the most palpable realities of life, and who is constantly taken by surprise in the circumstances with which he is familiar. But it may be advanced with confidence that the existence of a great republic will always be exposed to far greater perils than that of a small one.

"All the passions which are most fatal to republican institutions spread with an increase of territory, whilst the virtues which maintain their dignity do not augment in the same proportion."

After calling attention to a number of dangers that threaten an expanding empire, De Tocqueville says: "It may therefore be asserted as a general proposition that nothing is more opposed to the well-being and the freedom of man than vast empires."[1] These words were never so appropriate and pointed as now. Well may the American people heed them in their search for legal authority when their most vital need is security for personal freedom.

[1] *Democracy in America*, p. 159 *et seq.*

CHAPTER V

THE THEORY OF INTERNAL IMPROVEMENTS

THE problem of internal improvements was an important one that, by the logic of circumstances, had to arise in the course of the development of the United States. The rapid development of the country at the beginning of the nineteenth century naturally attracted attention to the advisability of resorting to state and Federal support for such purposes. The national debt resulting mainly from the Revolutionary War kept this question in the background for a few years after the establishment of the Federal Government, but by the beginning of Jefferson's administration it was seen that the increasing revenues would enable the authorities to meet all outstanding obligations as they came due, and by December, 1806, there was a substantial surplus in the national treasury. This immediately created the problem of the wise expenditure of our rapidly increasing national surplus.

When Congress convened in December, 1806, Jefferson sent a message[1] to Congress, recommend-

[1] *Annals of Congress*, December, 1806; President's message.

ing a policy that was both natural and appropriate to such a state of affairs. He recommended that Congress keep up the Federal impost, and that the accruing surpluses thereafter be used for the general welfare, which should include Federal aid to education, the construction of new roads and canals, and the improvement of river navigation on interior rivers and streams. Jefferson saw in his scheme of internal improvement great possibilities for the future good of the country.

"I experience [he said] great satisfaction at seeing my country proceed to facilitate the inter-communication of its several parts, by opening rivers, canals, and roads. How much more rational is this disposal of public money than that of waging war.

"I would propose a constitutional amendment for authority to apply the surplus taxes to objects of internal improvement.

"The fondest wish of my heart ever was that the surplus portion of these taxes, destined for the payment of the Revolutionary debt, should, when that object was accomplished, be continued by annual or biennial reënactment and applied, in times of peace, to the improvement of our country by canals, roads, and useful institutions, literary or others."[1]

In the furtherance of this scheme Gallatin, Jefferson's Secretary of the Treasury, began to draw up the specifications of the plan,[2] and on

[1] Curtis's *The True Thomas Jefferson*, p. 297.
[2] For the complete details of this plan see Adams's *Gallatin*, p. 351.

April 12, 1808, he sent to the Senate his elaborate proposal, which provided for canals, turnpike roads connecting the East with the West, and the improvement of the waterways in every section of the country. The scheme included a national university, and had it been carried out, it would have consumed all the surplus revenues for a decade or more.

The President believed firmly that an amendment to the Constitution would be necessary to carry out this undertaking, for no such specific power had been delegated to the Congress by the people in the Constitution, and the general grant "to make all laws which shall be necessary and proper for carrying into execution the foregoing [those specified in section 8] powers" could not relate to any new grants because such powers were not expressed in set terms. This was the conclusion reached by Jefferson on the subject, but Congress, encouraged by the flattering financial condition of the national treasury, and without seriously considering the constitutional objections, proceeded to create the Coast Survey, and made an appropriation for the Cumberland Road to extend from the Potomac to the Ohio River, and which was later to become a national highway penetrating the West across the Alleghany Mountains.

One of the early champions of this legislation by Congress was Henry Clay, of Kentucky, who had just entered the United States Senate to fill out an unexpired term of four months. He was naturally favorable to the appropriation of funds for the Cumberland Road, and at this time (February 28, 1807), he succeeded in securing the passage of a bill in the Senate appropriating a large amount of the national domain for the construction of a canal around the falls of the Ohio River, but the bill was not considered by the House.[1] Clay was elected a member of the House in 1811, and served in this capacity, with only one or two brief periods, until he entered the cabinet of John Quincy Adams as Secretary of State in 1825. During this period he supported and defended all the bills that were introduced in Congress relating to internal improvements, and when he re-entered the Senate he renewed his championship of these measures. He answered the constitutional objections of Jefferson and others by declaring the applicability of those passages that gave to Congress the power "to provide for the common defense," "to establish post roads," and "to pass laws necessary and proper for carrying into execution" the foregoing powers. Clay was supported in this doctrine by Calhoun and others, but he was the ablest and most conspicuous advocate of internal improvements, and he continued to support the doctrine until the end of his public career in 1850—two years before his death. Congress throughout this period had been generally favorable to this kind of legislation, but most of

[1] See Lalor's *Cyclopædia of Political Science*, vol. ii., p. 571.

the bills relating to this subject met with executive veto on constitutional grounds.

The early acts of Congress relating to this subject had set a precedent for applying the doctrine of implied powers to internal improvements and setting aside all constitutional limitations. It is interesting to conjecture what the result would have been had this question been adjudicated by the Supreme Court at this time. But the nature of the legislation made it impossible to become a matter at issue between litigant parties, and we can, therefore, only surmise. However, we are reminded that Marshall had been Chief Justice seven years at this time, and he had already indicated his future course in his decision in the case of Marbury v. Madison. But perhaps another consideration may even better enable us to forecast what might have resulted. The viewpoints of Jefferson and Marshall on the theory of construction of the Constitution were diametrically opposed. Jefferson wanted to restrict the powers of the National Government in the interest of human liberty, and Marshall was bent upon enlarging the powers of the Government in the interests of justice and nationality. John Adams had appointed Marshall for the purpose of perpetuating and developing the Federal principle in our National Government, and Jefferson had antagonized Marshall and criticized the Court because of his opposition to this principle. This fact might have been an unconscious consideration had the question of internal improvements been passed up to the Supreme Court for an opinion on its constitutional merits.

But the precedent set by Congress was not destined to settle the question. The War of 1812, however, which involved large financial obligations, made internal improvement by the National Government impossible. This war had another effect that had a bearing on the question. The American success in the war caused the destruction of the Federalist party. This party had violently opposed the war, and the twenty-six delegates that attended the Hartford Convention came from its ranks. They denounced the "ruinous war" and formulated a number of amendments to the Constitution designed to restrict the power of the slave-holding states, to protect the commercial interests of the North, to make more difficult the admission of Western states, and "to check the succession of Virginia Presidents." The Convention was in session one month and on adjournment the delegates sent messengers with their demands to Washington, but the latter arrived just as the news of the victory of Jackson at New Orleans and the Peace of Ghent was received, and the rejoicing over this news made the defeat of the Federalist party complete and the Hartford envoys returned to New England totally discredited before the country. The Republicans were now in complete ascendency, and they did not believe that Congress had power to authorize appropriations for internal improvements had the war not exhausted the funds of the national treasury.

The rapid development of the West and the limited capital for the development of this new section of the country had brought the question of internal improvements to the front again in 1816, when President Madison in his last annual message to Congress urged that body to provide aid for roads and canals "such as would have the effect of drawing more closely together every section of the country." A few days later Calhoun introduced a bill which provided for the appropriation of the $1,500,000 which had been promised to the Government as a bonus for the establishment of the second national bank and the dividends derived from Government stock in the bank, for internal improvements. The measure was bitterly opposed in both branches of Congress, but it finally passed with a close margin. President Madison, however, who believed in spending the nation's money for internal improvements, as his message of the preceding December had shown, nevertheless vetoed the measure because he believed with Jefferson that the Constitution had not given Congress this power.

Monroe, Madison's successor, assumed the responsibilities of the Presidency on the day following the veto of Calhoun's Bonus Bill for internal improvements, and of course the subject was uppermost in the public mind at this time. Monroe felt called upon to consider the question in his first message to Congress, and in doing so he advised Congress to recommend to the states a constitutional amendment bestowing the power upon Congress to appropriate funds and to undertake internal improvements. "Disregarding early impressions," he declared, "I have bestowed on the subject all the deliberation which its great importance and a just sense of my duty required, and the result is a settled conviction in my mind that Congress does not possess the right."

The advice of Monroe was accepted by the Senate, and an attempt was made to submit an amendment to the state legislatures with this object in view, but opposition developed, and in the House there was a noticeable unwillingness to await the delay that such a procedure would involve. Three resolutions were introduced in the House each asserting that Congress already had such power, but each in turn was defeated. But the discussion resulting from these resolutions brought out an important distinction that looked to the practical solution of the difficulty. It was explained that the power to originate works of internal improvement by national authority and the right simply to appropriate funds to aid construction already begun by the states were very different matters, and it was the belief of many that Congress had power under the latter condition. The question was thus disposed of with the requirement that the Secretaries of war and the

Treasury make an investigation to determine what improvements were under way in the various states and report at the next session of Congress.

The request was complied with, and at the opening of the Fifteenth Congress a full report was laid before that body. But an empty treasury made it impossible to carry out the recommendations made, with the exception of providing a half million dollars for the extension of the Cumberland Road to the Ohio River. This was the beginning of a political fight which was destined to continue with slight interruptions for the next twenty years, with such national leaders as Clay and Adams on the one side, and Jackson, whose political ascendency was just beginning, on the other.

But the short lull resulting from the depletion of the treasury was to be followed shortly by renewed persistency for national appropriations for internal improvements. Every section and state was anxious to promote its material advancement and every community was interested in some kind of internal improvement for which national aid was sought, and nothing was more popular than to advocate liberal expenditure from the treasury for these various objects of local interest. It was easy to see that national interest and welfare were in danger of being lost sight of in the great concern for local interest and provincial advantage, and Monroe was quick to perceive this danger.

8

Monroe sought an opportunity to recall to the representatives of the people the constitutional principle involved, and the opportunity came when a bill was passed by Congress in 1822, appropriating the small sum of $9000 for the repair of the Cumberland Road, and authorizing in addition the erection of tollgates and the collection of tolls for keeping the road in repair. Monroe returned the bill with his veto, the attempt to pass the measure over his opposition failed, and the bill was lost. The President accompanied his veto message with a state paper in which he gave his views on the subject. The statement must for all time take rank as one of the best papers ever written by a President. This document had been prepared and submitted to his cabinet in 1819, but at the request of Adams, Calhoun, and Crawford, who were not in harmony with his views on the subject, it was not sent to Congress.[1] He reviewed at great length the clauses of the Federal Constitution under which loose constructionists claimed the right of Congress to appropriate money for internal improvements, and showed that in each case the interpretations were untenable. He did accede to the opinion of Congress, expressed in 1818, that Congress could appropriate money in aid of internal improvements already begun by the several states. The effect of this paper was to defeat temporarily the advocates of this popular policy.

[1] Schouler's *History of the United States*, vol. iv., p. 254.

The succeeding administration tried to sweep over the precedent established by Monroe, but this policy was not approved, for public opinion was gradually yielding to the logic of the President's argument.

The question of internal improvements was one of the few great political issues before the people that have never been reviewed by the Supreme Court, but Monroe's veto gave the members of the Court a chance to express an opinion on the subject. The incident is one of the most interesting and unusual in our political history. Monroe sent a copy of his veto message to each member of the Supreme Court, and Justice Johnson[1] replied in a very important communication. He intimated that the bank decision (M'Cullough v. State of Maryland) in the opinion of his associates on the Bench committed the tribunal to the doctrine of internal improvement by national appropriations in so far as they applied to post roads and military roads; but on the other points the argument of Monroe carried conviction. No opinion was expressed by Story on the matter.

[1] William Johnson, of South Carolina, was appointed to the Supreme Bench by Jefferson, and previous to the time of his appointment had been an ardent admirer of Jefferson, but on account of a criticism resulting from some decision while acting as circuit judge, he became less friendly to Jefferson. The tendency of Johnson on constitutional questions had been that of a mild Federalist. He rarely approved of the views on nationality held by Marshall, and he resented the extreme views maintained by Story.

The Chief Justice in his reply said that "it is a subject on which many divide in opinion; but all will admit that your views are profound and that you have thought much on the subject." But further than this he did not go, believing no doubt that it would be inappropriate for the Court to express an opinion on a mere political question.

John Quincy Adams became President in 1825, and internal improvement under national direction was the central object of the domestic policy advocated by him, and his first message to Congress exceeded all previous declarations on the subject. He proposed governmental aid, not only to roads and canals, "but to seminaries of science and learning, observatories, and expeditions." He went so far as to cause even Clay to doubt the wisdom of his message on this subject, and both Wirt and Barbour, members of his cabinet, objected to his taking such strong ground on internal improvements. Later Adams himself admitted that he went too far in his message.[1] But conflicting interests of the various sections of the country had already directed the attention of Congress to other matters, and very little was done along the line of internal improvement during the administration of Adams.

During the administration of Adams the two wings of the Republican party drew so far apart as to make necessary new names to designate them. The followers of Adams and Clay, whose most

[1] Shouler's *History of the United States*, vol. iv., p. 358.

distinct and prominent doctrine was internal improvement at national expense, were called National-Republicans; and the opponents of this policy, under the leadership of Jackson, Calhoun, and Crawford, were called by the original party name of Democratic-Republicans. The former, without changing essentially their party beliefs, developed into the Whig party, and the latter likewise became the Democratic party. We shall now see how the doctrine of internal improvement continued as a party issue with these new alignments.

In 1828 Adams, the candidate of the National-Republican party, was defeated for reëlection by Andrew Jackson, his Democratic opponent. The question of internal improvement was thrust upon him by Congress. Several bills were passed which he tried to persuade his friends in Congress to defeat, but to no avail. The first of these was the Maysville and Lexington Turnpike bill, which he returned to the House with his veto, and it was lost. Of the four other bills passed just before the close of the session, he approved one, vetoed one, and defeated the other two by retaining them until after adjournment. This was the beginning of Jackson's famous exercise of the veto power.

Jackson gave as his reasons for opposing legislation dealing with internal improvements that such improvements should wait until the national debt was paid, and the Constitution amended so that power could be vested in Congress.[1] The friends of internal improvement protested bitterly against Jackson's veto of these measures, but the policy on the whole proved to be popular, especially in the South. The teaching of Monroe on the subject had helped at this time to justify the position of Jackson.

Clay was the National-Republican opponent of Jackson in 1832, and his was the first platform ever adopted by any party in this country. The third resolution reads as follows: "A uniform system of internal improvements, sustained and supported by the general government, is calculated to secure, in the highest degree, the harmony, the strength, and the permanency of the republic." The doctrine of the Democrats was not expressed on this subject in a platform until 1840, when this language was used: "The Constitution does not confer upon the general government the power to commence and carry on a general system of internal improvements." This doctrine was reaffirmed in each succeeding Democratic platform until 1860.

The question of internal improvements began

[1] Jackson, five years earlier, while a member of the Senate, had repeatedly voted in favor of bills for internal improvement, but his convictions had undergone a change, which were partly due to political considerations and partly due to his fear of the dominating influence of the moneyed interests. His belief in strict construction had also deepened, but he was never greatly influenced by technical constitutional constructions. (See Dewey's *Financial History of the United States*, p. 215.)

to give way gradually after 1832 in the presence of other questions of growing importance—the political issues connected with the rechartering of the United States Bank, the tariff, and the annexation of Texas; and all of these were destined to give way shortly to the absorbing and paramount question of slavery.[1] An echo of the internal improvement controversy was heard during the financial troubles of Van Buren's administration when the Whigs charged that the financial distress had been largely brought on by the refusal of the Government to lend its aid to internal improvement.

In the campaign of 1840 the last echo of the doctrine of internal improvement was heard in the promises of the Whigs to secure the passage of internal improvement bills should that party win at the polls. The Whigs did not adopt a platform in that year and no formal declaration was made, and their mere party promises did not mature when Harrison and Tyler, the Whig candidates, won the election. But the death of Harrison early in his administration, and the weak party faith of Tyler in the Whig party beliefs may have had something to do with the failure of these

[1] Gradually it began to be realized by the several states that Federal aid for internal improvements was to be greatly restricted, and the state legislatures began to assume this responsibility. Previous to 1820 the states had incurred practically no liability for this purpose, but in the decade—1830–1840—the total exceeded $200,000,000. (See Bogard's *Economic History of the United States*, p. 214.)

campaign promises to be fulfilled, but after all the day had passed for much legislation in the interest of internal improvements.

Concluding Observations

The political issue of internal improvements presents two or three very interesting phases because of which it deserves a brief survey. In the first place, it is one of the few great national issues that never really came up to the Supreme Court for constitutional affirmation or denial. The nearest approach to it came in the administration of Monroe when he attempted to get an opinion of the Court on his own analysis of the doctrine, and the remarks of Justice Johnson represent the only committal words that we have from the Supreme Court touching the issue.

In the second place, no other issue of national importance has ever been so influenced by the rise and fall of our national resources. In the language of Schouler[1]:

" No theme for public agitation in this era of our history seems to have swelled and died away with the ebb and flow of the National Treasury like that of internal improvements. . . . Like an organ whose keyboard emits no sound until air is forced into the pipes, nothing was heard of this policy while the revenues were exhausted; but now, when the national debt decreased and confi-

[1] *History of the United States*, vol. iv., p. 249.

dence revived, the diapason swelled into a loud acclaim for great national works, to be prosecuted at the cost of the whole Union."

This was characteristic of the history of the whole agitation. In the third place, we can hardly avoid a speculation that obtrudes itself in the study of the history of this issue. While the whole question of internal improvement was uppermost in the public mind, there began the construction of the first railroads under private initiative in this country. The Mohawk and Hudson Company began in 1825, and two years later the Boston and Albany and the Pennsylvania. The construction of the Baltimore and Ohio was undertaken in 1828. Canals had been the chief object of construction at national expense, with the exception of roads, and these railroads naturally began to supersede the canals as an agency of transportation. It is remarkable that the public did not immediately see the possibilities of railroads and start a movement designed to construct them at national expense. Professor Muzzey[1] makes an interesting comment on this possibility.

" Who can calculate the effect on the economic and political history of our country if the construction and management of railways had been adopted as part of the national government's business in John Quincy Adams' administration, and if Congress now had the same control over

[1] *American History*, p. 266.

the steel lines of land transportation that it has over the rivers and harbors of the United States."

The status of the doctrine at the present time may be summarized as follows. The right of Congress to appropriate money for lighthouses, buoys, beacons, and public piers has since 1789 been recognized as being within the expressed power of Congress. The first actual appropriation for other internal improvement was for the construction of the Cumberland Road in 1806. In May, 1822, President Monroe vetoed the Cumberland Road bill, and gave to the world at the same time his famous state paper on the same subject, in which he denied that Congress had constitutional power to pass such measures. Congress passed the first act for harbor improvement in 1823. Jackson in 1830 vetoed the Maysville Turnpike Road bill, which had the effect of removing all question as to the power of Congress to authorize such expenditure. Since that time all such improvements have been regarded as the legitimate objects of expenditure on the part of the individual states.[1]

[1] See *Dictionary of American History*, vol. i., p. 351.

CHAPTER VI

THEORY OF THE UNITED STATES BANK

THE history of banking in this country can be traced back to 1714, when a land bank, modeled, no doubt, from ideas obtained from John Law of France, was established in Boston. Loans were to be made on ratable estates equal to two-thirds their value. The scheme proved very popular with a large class of people. But the bank was attacked by Paul Dudley, Attorney-General, on certain legal grounds, and when the matter of granting a charter to the institution came before the assembly of the colony, it was refused. The land bank of 1741 was the next to be established, but its methods of doing business almost produced a revolution.[1] But in spite of popular opposition, many new banks began to spring up, and our commercial affairs were threatened with an experience not dissimilar to that of the English South Sea speculative mania, which had the effect of causing the country in later times to distrust banks and banking schemes.

National banking in the United States had its inception in the creation of the Bank of North

[1] Dewey's *Financial History of the United States*, p. 25.

America at Philadelphia. This bank grew out of the plan of Robert Morris, Superintendent of Finance, who established the bank in the hope of redeeming the depreciated bills of credit issued by Congress during the Revolutionary War. The charter was granted by Congress in 1782. As serious doubts existed as to the authority of Congress to charter a bank under the Articles of Confederation, the bank took out a charter under the laws of Pennsylvania. This bank was regarded as a state bank by Hamilton, and it was generally regarded as such, until our National Banking law went into effect in 1863, when it took out a charter under the laws of the United States. It is still in existence, and has the distinction of being the oldest banking institution in the United States.

In Hamilton's great report to Congress on December 13, 1790, he recommended the establishment of a United States Bank. In this report he set forth with much acumen the nature and function of the bank. A bill was immediately introduced in Congress in conformity to the recommendation of the Secretary of the Treasury. The bill was strenuously opposed, Madison leading the opposition, on the ground "That the power of establishing an incorporated bank was not among the powers vested in Congress by the Constitution." However, the majority accepted the doctrine of loose construction and on February 25, 1791, the bill became a law.

A provision in this law limited the existence of the bank to twenty years. At the expiration of that term, although the bank had prospered, when the stockholders applied for a renewal of the charter, a bitter controversy arose. Secretary Gallatin recommended a renewal of the charter with an increase of the bank's capital. The fact that 18,000 shares of the stock of the bank were held by foreigners, and the intense antagonism of our people toward England at this time, had much to do with the final result. Clay, who had come into prominence at this time, opposed the bank on the ground that "the Constitution did not originally authorize Congress to grant the charter"; therefore, the renewal would be unconstitutional. Clay, in later life, became the bank's greatest champion. It is claimed by many that Clay's later views never successfully answered his own argument in this earlier period.[1] Largely through Clay's influence the charter was defeated in the House by the decisive vote of 165 to 64. The vote in the Senate was a tie, but Vice-President George Clinton cast his vote against it, and the charter failed of renewal.

An unforeseen condition arose soon after the closing of the first bank that made possible the creation of the second national bank. There sprang up throughout the country a great number of irresponsible state banks. State laws on the subject were not uniform, and in many cases they

[1] See Calwell's *Henry Clay*, p. 26.

were so loosely drawn as to allow wild-cat banking. The country was flooded with cheap paper money. National finances were in a chaotic condition. The friends of the first United States Bank considered this a result of the failure to recharter the Bank. Clay was away during a part of 1814–1815, as a Peace Commissioner. But upon his return he confessed that his views had undergone a change. His biographers assert that this was the only change of political view that he ever made on any great measure. Surely he was gradually shifting his view at this time from strict to loose construction. Madison had also shifted his view on this subject. He likewise had been opposed to the first bank on constitutional grounds; but the chaotic financial conditions caused him, when he became President, to send a message to Congress in 1815 recommending a national bank to meet the financial problem of the Federal Government. In conformity with this recommendation, a bill was introduced, and on April 16, 1816, the bill was passed, and on January 7, 1817, the bank opened for business.

While many had been induced to support the national bank on grounds of expediency, still there was a general belief that the act was not supported by any provision of the Constitution and that Congress had exceeded its power. Two years after the passage of the act, the Supreme Court handed down its great decision in the case of M'Cullough *v.* State of Maryland *et al.*,[1] which supported the theory of the constitutionality of the act in the strongest terms. This case grew out of the passage of a statute in 1818 by the Legislature of Maryland, assessing a tax on "all banks or branches thereof in the State of Maryland not chartered by the Legislature." M'Cullough, the cashier, had violated this law by refusing to use the stamped paper in making notes as required. Chief Justice Marshall delivered the opinion of the Court. After raising the question as to the right of Congress to incorporate a bank, the Court proceeded to affirm the power, as follows:

"It has been truly said, that this can scarcely be considered an open question, entirely unprejudiced by the former proceeding of the Nation respecting it. The principle now contested was introduced at a very early period of our history, has been recognized by many successive legislatures, and has been acted upon by the judicial department, in cases of peculiar delicacy, as a law of undoubted obligation.

" The power now contested was exercised by the first Congress elected under the present Constitution. The bill for creating the Bank of the United States did not steal upon an unsuspecting legislature and pass unobserved. Its principle was completely understood, and was opposed with equal zeal and ability. After being resisted, first in the fair and open field of debate, and afterward in the executive cabinet, with as much persevering talent as any measure has ever experienced, and being

[1] 4 Wheaton, 316.

supported by arguments which convinced minds as pure and as intelligent as this country can boast, it became a law. The original act was permitted to expire; but a short experience of the embarrassment to which the refusal to revive it exposed the Government, convinced those who were most prejudiced against the measure of its necessity, and induced the passage of the present law. It would require no ordinary share of intrepidity to assert, that a measure adopted under these conditions, was a bold and plain usurpation, to which the Constitution gave no countenance."

The Court then answered the argument of counsel for the State of Maryland who contended that ratification of the Constitution was the individual act of the sovereign states. The Court denied this by asserting that ratification was the sovereign act of the people of the several states, and concluded this part of the argument as follows:

"The Government of the Union, then (whatever may be the influence of this fact on the case), is emphatically and truly a Government of the people. In form and substance it emanates from them, its powers are granted by them, and are to be exercised directly on them, and for their benefit."

The Court then proceeded to apply the doctrine of loose construction to the matter under consideration.

" Among the enumerated powers, we do not find that of establishing a bank or creating a corporation. But there is no phrase in the instrument which, like the Articles of Confederation, excludes incidental or implied powers; and which requires that everything granted shall be expressly and minutely described. A constitution to contain an accurate detail of all the subdivisions of which its great powers will admit, and of all the means by which they may be carried out, would partake of the prolixity of a legal code, and could scarcely be embraced by the human mind. Although, among the enumerated powers of Government, we do not find the word 'bank' or 'incorporation,' we find the great powers to lay and collect taxes; to borrow money; to regulate commerce; to declare and conduct a war; and to raise and support armies and navies. It may with great reason be contended, that a government, intrusted with such powers, on the due execution of which the happiness and prosperity of the nation depends, must also be intrusted with ample means for their execution. The power being given, it is the interest of the nation to facilitate its execution. It can never be their interest, and cannot be presumed to have been their intention to clog and embarrass its execution by withholding the most appropriate means. But the Constitution of the United States has not left the right of Congress to employ the necessary means, for the execution of the powers conferred on the Government, to general reasoning. To its enumerated powers is added that of making 'all laws which shall be necessary and proper, for carrying into execution the foregoing powers, and all other powers vested by this Constitution in the Government of the United States, or in any department thereof.'"

The Court concludes by saying that

9

"After the most deliberate consideration, it is the unanimous and decided opinion of this Court, that the act to incorporate the Bank of the United States is a law made in pursuance of the Constitution, and is a part of the supreme law of the land."

In 1824, the Supreme Court sustained their decision in M'Cullough *v.* State of Maryland in the case of Osborn *v.* the United States Bank.[1] This decision is important, not only in sustaining the constitutionality of the bank, but also in its very careful analysis of the nature of the bank as a Federal corporation. The Court was called upon to pass on seven questions, the last of which was that of the constitutionality of a state law which imposed a tax on one of the branches of the Bank of the United States. After referring to the case M'Cullough *v.* State of Maryland, the Court said:

"A revision of that opinion has been requested; and many conditions combine to induce a review of it. The foundation of the argument in favor of the right of a State to tax the bank, is laid in the supposed character of the institution. The argument supposes the corporation to have been originated for the management of an individual concern, to be founded upon contract between individuals, having private trade and private profit for its great end and principal object. If these premises were true, the conclusion drawn would be inevitable. This mere private corporation, engaging in its own business, with its own views, would certainly be subject to

[1] 9 Wheaton, 738.

the taxing power of the State, as any individual would be; and the casual circumstance of its being employed by the Government in the transaction of its fiscal affairs, would no more exempt its private business from the operation of that power, than it would exempt the private business of any individual employed in the same manner. But the premises are not true. The bank is not considered as a private corporation, whose principal object is individual trade and individual profit; but a public corporation, created for public and national purposes. It was not created for its own sake, or for private purposes. It has never been supposed that Congress could create such a corporation. The whole opinion of the Court in M'Cullough v. State of Maryland is founded on, and sustained by, the idea that the bank is an instrument which is 'necessary and proper for carrying into effect the powers vested in the Government of the United States.' It is not an instrument which the Government found ready made, and has supposed to be adapted to its purposes; but one which was created in the form in which it now appears, for national purposes only. It is, undoubtedly, capable of transacting private as well as public business. While it is the great instrument by which the fiscal operations of the Government are effected, it is also trading with individuals for its own advantage. The appellants endeavored to distinguish between this trade and its agency for the public, between its banking operations and those qualities which it possesses in common with every corporation, such as individuality, immortality, etc. While they seem to admit the right to preserve this corporate existence, they deny the right to protect it in its trade and business.

"If there be anything in this distinction, it would tend to show that so much of the act as incorporates the bank is constitutional, but so much of it as authorizes its banking operations is unconstitutional. Congress can make the inanimate body, and employ the machinery as a depository of, and vehicle for, the conveyance of the treasure of the Nation, if it be capable of being so employed, but cannot breathe into it the vital spirit which alone can bring it into useful existence."

The Court then proceeded to show the essential unity in the bank's double function.

"Why is it that Congress can incorporate or create a bank? This question was answered in the case of M'Cullough v. the State of Maryland. It is an instrument which is 'necessary and proper' for carrying on the fiscal operations of the Government. Can this instrument, on any rational calculation, effect its object, unless it be endowed with that faculty of lending and dealing in money which is conferred by its charter? If it can, if it be as competent to the purposes of Government without, as with this faculty, there will be much difficulty in sustaining that essential part of the charter. If it cannot, then this faculty is necessary to the legitimate operations of Government, and was constitutionally and rightfully engrafted on the institution."

The Court then proceeds to prove that the lending and dealing in money is the "vital part," the very soul of the institution.

"Deprive a bank of its trade and business, which is its sustenance, and its immortality, if it have that property, will be a very useless attribute. This distinction then has no real existence. To tax its faculties, its trade, and occupation, is to tax the bank itself. To destroy or preserve one, is to destroy or preserve the other."

This decision was hailed by the friends of the bank with delight. It had recognized the right of Congress to create an institution which could serve the Government's financial needs unhampered by any restrictions in its private functions as a banking corporation. But political changes were gradually being effected which were to have a wonderful influence in shaping the affairs of the bank.

Andrew Jackson was just beginning to attract the attention of the nation when the decision in the case of Osborn *v.* the United States Bank was handed down. In his campaign for the Presidency in 1828, the bank was not an issue. Jackson was opposed by Adams and the issue between them was a personal one. It was simply a question of whether Adams was a good man, who merited reëlection, or whether Jackson was the true representative of the American people. Jackson was elected, and very soon after his election he began to manifest that aggressive policy that has made his administration one of the most notable in the history of the country. He gave notice that he would, at the proper time, oppose the recharter of the United States Bank. When the bill to recharter finally came to him, he vetoed it, taking issue in his veto message with the Supreme Court on the constitutionality of the bank. He followed in the footsteps of Jefferson and held that a bank was neither necessary nor proper, and that for Congress to attempt to effect such legislation was a plain transgression of power. But in the argument advanced in this message,[1] Jackson used a novel theory as to the mode of construction of our organic law; quite at variance with that accepted and promulgated by the Supreme Court.

" Each public officer [said he] who takes an oath to support the Constitution, swears that he will support it as he understands it and not as it is understood by others. The opinion of the judges has no more authority over Congress than the opinion of Congress has over the judges, and on that point the President is independent of both. The authority of the Supreme Court must not, therefore, be permitted to control Congress or the Executive when acting in their legislative capacities, but to have only such influence as the force of their reasoning may deserve."

The obvious result of this doctrine would be to bestow upon the President or Congress the right to pass upon the constitutionality of an act, and to give either the same weight as that bestowed upon the Supreme Court. According to Jackson's theory he had the right to deny the constitutionality of the bank with an authority equal to that of the Supreme Court in affirming it.

[1] See Veto Message of July 10, 1832.

In his message of 1829 Jackson claimed also that the bank had "failed in the great end of establishing a uniform and sound currency." The bank had also suffered some loss of prestige, due to the mismanagement of its officials, but when this condition came to the attention of the directors, they removed those officials from office, and placed the bank's affairs in competent hands. In opposition to the attack made by Jackson, the leaders of the National-Republican party, among these being Webster and Clay, rallied to the bank's support. With this alignment, the bank became the chief issue in the campaign of 1832. Jackson was reëlected, and through his influence the bill to recharter was defeated. The bank then took out a state charter and continued business until 1841 when it failed.

The verdict of Congress and the attitude of the President did not convince an able minority in Congress and a large number of the people outside of Congress of the wisdom of the course. The earlier attitude of the Supreme Court had convinced many that the constitutionality of the bank was beyond question, and that the issue could only be one of expediency or economic policy. Many thought the bank should on these grounds be rechartered. The Democratic party took the opposite view and consistently opposed the bank for the next thirty years. The Democratic platform of 1836 (which was really not a platform in the modern sense, but a party declaration made by the Democrats of New York, and conceded to be the prevailing view of the party throughout the country) said: "We declare unqualified hostility to bank notes and paper money as circulating medium, because gold and silver is the only safe and constitutional currency; *hostility to any and all monopolies by legislation,* because they are violations of equal rights of all the people." Four years later, at the convention in Baltimore, where Van Buren was nominated for President, the Democratic platform had a more specific plank in opposition to the bank; the sixth resolution declared,

" that Congress had no power to charter a United States bank; that we believe such an institution one of deadly hostility to the best interests of the country, dangerous to our republican institutions and the liberties of the people; and calculated to place the business of the country within the control of a concentrated money power and above the laws and will of the people."

This resolution, in practically the same language, was incorporated in the Democratic platforms of 1852 and 1856.

In the early period of the bank controversy the Democrats were opposed by the National-Republicans. But about 1834 the Whigs came into existence as the opposers of Jackson and the Jackson policies. This party was destined to play an important part in the political history of the country from 1834 to 1856. "The Whigs were never a party of fixed principles and harmonious purpose." The party had its origin in the general opposition to Jackson, and its attempt to unite in one political party all the factions antagonistic to Jackson made it impossible to secure support through sound political principle and party consistency. The Whigs did not in any of their platforms declare in favor of the bank; but their opposition to Jackson, their nomination of Clay in 1844 for the Presidency, and the public utterances of their party leaders, reveal the general sympathy of the party for the bank. This was the status of the question at the beginning of the Civil War.

Out of the exigencies of the Civil War arose the real solution of the bank question. To meet the financial demands of the war, the Government was compelled both to borrow money directly and to issue bonds. To create a demand for the bonds, Secretary Chase, Treasurer of the United States, proposed that certain banking privileges should be offered to aid the sale of the bonds. In conformity to the recommendations of Secretary Chase, Congress, in February, 1863, passed the National Banking Act. This act never became the subject of attack on constitutional grounds. The United States banks had been opposed principally because they were monopolies created by legislation and "calculated to place the business of the country within the control of a concentrated money power." The act of 1863 was free from this objection, as the banking was to be under private direction with only a Federal regulation.

But with the passage of the National Banking Act of 1863, the bank question was to take a new form. The interest of the banks under Federal regulation was destined to come into conflict with the state banks over the country. The nature of the conflict is briefly described by a leading authority[1] as follows:

"The fiscal advantages of the national banking system were equally important and enduring. For the uncertainties of seven thousand varieties of State bank notes issued by fifteen hundred private banks that were chartered by twenty-nine State legislatures of varying financial proclivities, was substituted a uniform currency whose redemption was guaranteed by bonds of the United States. The State banks could make but a losing fight against such odds."

But in addition to this advantage, Congress, to give a deathblow to the circulation of state bank notes, on March 3, 1865, passed a law placing a tax of ten per cent. per annum upon the state issues of bank notes. The national banks were made to some extent the depositories of the public funds. Naturally those interested in the state banks were violently opposed to the act of 1865. The right of Congress to enact this law was strenuously denied. It was believed to be an

[1] Coman's *Industrial History of the United States*, p. 271.

invasion of state authority.[1] The question was destined to be settled by the Supreme Court before it became a matter for serious party difference. On December 13, 1869, the question of the con- stitutionality of this tax was decided in the case of Veazie Bank v. Fenno[2] in a brief but important decision. The plaintiff's brief in denying this power to Congress was very strong. Among other points made in the brief was the following:

" We insist, further, that the tax excepted to in this case is unconstitutional on the following grounds: It is not a tax imposed for the sake of revenue. Its excessive character, which is made evident by the reference to the tax imposed on the circulation of the national banks already cited, proves that the true purpose of this tax is to destroy the State banks.

" If Congress, by discriminating taxation, can destroy the State banks, it can equally, in the same manner, destroy the railroad system of the States."

Attorney-General Hoar answered for the defendant, touching these points as follows:

" Congress would have the constitutional right to prohibit what it thus undertakes to tax, and whatever it may prohibit (non malum in se), it may regulate or permit upon condition. If Congress has the power to tax, the degree of taxation is not to be regarded by this Court, but is within

---

[1] See Hawthorne-Schouler-Andrew, *Hist. of U. S.*, vol. vii., pp. 282 *et seq.*   [2] 18 Wallace, 482.

the discretion of Congress, the motive of which cannot be inquired into within the scope of its constitutional function. The power to tax includes the power to make taxation burdensome or even destructive to particular branches of business."

Chief Justice Chase delivered the opinion of the Court, and it is a significant fact that he had, before coming to the Bench, been the most important factor in effecting the legislation now under consideration. After tracing the history of Congressional legislation to show that there had been previously a tendency to "discriminate for, rather than against, the circulation of state banks," the Court then declared that when the country had been sufficiently furnished with a national currency by the issue of United States notes, the discrimination had been turned decidedly in the opposite direction. The Court then raised and proceeded to answer two questions: (1) Is this a direct tax and has it been apportioned among the several states agreeably to the Constitution? This question was answered in the affirmative. (2) Is an act imposing a tax which impairs a franchise granted by a state, a power granted to Congress within the meaning of the Constitution? The Court said on this point,

"that it cannot be admitted that franchises granted by a State are necessarily exempt from taxation; for franchises are property, often very valuable and productive property; and when not conferred for the purpose of giving effect to some reserved power of a State, seem to be as properly objects of taxation as any other property. It is insisted, however, that the tax in the case before us is excessive, and so excessive as to indicate on the part of Congress a purpose to destroy the franchise of the bank, and is, therefore, beyond the constitutional power of Congress. The first answer is that the judicial cannot prescribe to the legislative department of the Government limitations upon the exercise of its acknowledged powers. But there is another answer which vindicates equally the wisdom and power of Congress. It cannot be doubted that under the Constitution the power to provide a circulating medium of coin is given to Congress. And it is settled by the uniform practice of the Government, and by repeated discussions, that Congress may constitutionally authorize the emission of bills of credit. Having thus, in the exercise of undisputed constitutional powers, undertaken to provide a currency for the whole country, it cannot be questioned that Congress may, constitutionally, secure the benefit of it to the people by appropriate legislation. To this end, Congress has denied the quality of legal tender to foreign coins, and has provided by law against the imposition of counterfeit and base coin on the community. To the same end, Congress may restrain, by suitable enactments, the circulation as money of any notes not issued under its own authority."

Justice Nelson gave a dissenting opinion in this case that was not answered in the majority opinion, and which could hardly be controverted. On the second point under consideration he said:

"The constitutional authority of the State to create these institutions, and to invest them with full banking powers, is hardly denied. But it may be useful to recur for a few moments to the source of this authority. The Tenth Amendment to the Constitution is as follows: 'The powers not delegated to the United States by the Constitution, nor prohibited by it to the States, are reserved to the States respectively.' On looking into the Constitution, it will be found that there is no clause or provision which, either expressly or by reasonable implication, delegates this power to the Federal Government, which originally belonged to the States, nor which prohibits it to them. In the discussion of the subject of the creation of the first Bank of the United States, in the First Congress, and in the cabinet of Washington, in 1790 and 1791, no question was made as to the constitutionality of the State banks. The only doubt that existed, and which divided the opinion of the most eminent statesmen of the day, many of whom had just largely participated in the formation of the Constitution, the Government under which they were then engaged in organizing, was, whether or not Congress possessed a concurrent power to incorporate a banking institution of the United States."

Justice Nelson concluded by saying that the effect of this decision would be to put the state banks out of business. The immediate effect was to declare practically that state banks were unconstitutional, because it was generally believed that the function of issuing a circulating medium was a necessary attribute of a bank.

With this decision the bank as a political issue came to an end. There will doubtless be bank issues in the future, but they will be based on economic policy rather than on constitutional principle. The bank controversy had the effect of furnishing the subject-matter from which the judiciary has planted deeply the doctrine of implied powers, as well as of stimulating thought out of which there has evolved a financial system of wonderful efficiency. Time has proved that in spite of an occasional abuse of power the fears of its opponents that it would result in a monopolistic money power have proved groundless. It is the universal opinion of the leaders of all political parties that the banks, as they are organized to-day, are among the greatest agencies in the up-building of the nation.

CHAPTER VII

THEORY OF LEGAL TENDER

ONE of the earliest problems that confronted the colonists was that of providing a stable medium of exchange to meet the demands of an expanding trade. There was not a sufficient amount of gold and silver to pay for the commodities brought over from England. The largest amount of specie came from the West Indies and other southern Spanish colonies, which was received from the sale of lumber, salt fish, etc., but this trade did not bring in sufficient coin to supply the demand for a medium of exchange. Mints were established in several colonies, but even this did not solve the difficulty. It was necessary, even then, to use many staple articles such as tobacco, corn, etc., as a medium to facilitate trade. But it is probable that the first substitute for coin to be used was the Indian "wampum," which was a shell that passed as money among the Indians, and which was made use of by the colonists in their trade with the Indian tribes. We learn from Hutchinson's *History of Massachusetts* that bills of credit were first emitted in that colony in 1690.

Soon after this we find most of the colonies issuing bills of credit, but in evidence of unsatisfactory results, laws were soon passed to prevent the further issue of such bills.[1]

The right of the colonies to issue bills of credit was never seriously questioned by England, but such bills were denied circulation as legal tender by that country in payment for English commodities. But upon the breaking out of the Revolutionary War, some of the colonies, notably Massachusetts, ignored the prohibition of Parliament, and endowed their bills with the power of legal tender. With the deathblow to English supremacy in America, the colonies inherited full power to make their bills of credit legal tender within their own jurisdiction. In the meantime the colonies had delegated to the Continental Congress power to issue bills of credit in the following words: "The United States, in Congress assembled, shall have authority to borrow money or emit bills on the credit of the United States, transmitting every half year to the respective States an account of the sums of money so borrowed or emitted."[2] And Article XII. of this document says: "All bills of credit emitted, moneys borrowed, and debts contracted by or under the authority of Congress shall be a charge against the United States"; but the power to make these bills a legal tender was nowhere expressly given to Congress, and it is,

[1] See Coman's *Industrial History of the United States*, p. 83.
[2] Articles of Confederation, Article IX.

10

therefore, assumed that this power was reserved to the colonies.

The historical development of the legal tender theory was carefully traced in a learned opinion by Mr. Justice Bradley in Knox *v.* Lee and Parker *v.* Davis.[1]

"In this country, the habit had prevailed from the beginning of the eighteenth century, of using bills of credit; and the Revolution of Independence had just been achieved in great degree by the means of similar bills issued by the Continental Congress. These bills were generally made a legal tender for the payment of all debts, public and private, until, by the influence of the English merchants at home, Parliament prohibited the issue of bills with that quality. This prohibition was first exercised in 1751, against the New England colonies; and subsequently, in 1763, against all the colonies. It was one of the causes of discontent which finally culminated in the Revolution. Dr. Franklin endeavored to obtain a repeal of the prohibitory acts, but only succeeded in obtaining from Parliament, in 1773, an act authorizing the colonies to make their bills receivable for taxes and debts due to the colony that issued them. At the breaking out of the war, the Continental Congress commenced the issue of bills of credit, and the war was carried on without other resources for three or four years. It may be said with truth, that we owe our National Independence to the use of this fiscal agency. Dr. Franklin, in a letter dated from Paris, in April, 1779, after deploring the depreciation which the continental currency had undergone, said: 'The only conso-

[1] 12 Wallace, 315.

lation under the evil is, that the public debt is
proportionately diminished by the depreciation;
and this by a kind of imperceptible tax, every one
having paid a part of it in the fall of value that
took place between the receiving and paying such
sums as passed through his hands.' He adds:
'This effect of paper currency is not understood
on this side of the water. And, indeed, the whole
is a mystery even to the politicians, how we have
been able to continue a war four years without
money, and how we could pay with paper, that
had no previously fixed fund appropriated especially to redeem it. This currency, as we
manage it, is a wonderful machine. It performs
its office when we issue it; it pays and clothes
troops, and provides victuals and ammunition.'[1]
The continental bills were not made legal tender
at first, but in January, 1777, the Congress passed
resolutions declaring that they ought to pass
current in all payments, and be deemed in value
equal to the same nominal sums in Spanish
dollars, and that any one refusing so to receive
them ought to be deemed an enemy to the liberties of the United States; and recommending to
the legislatures of the several States to pass laws
to that effect.[2] Congress seems to have clearly
recognized the exclusive power of the colonies to
make bills of credit legal tender."

The Court, continuing, said:

"Massachusetts and other colonies, on the breaking out of the war, disregarded the prohibitions
of Parliament and again conferred upon their bills

[1] Franklin's *Works*, vol. viii., p. 329.
[2] *Journal of Congress*, volume iii., pp. 19 and 20. Pitkin's
History, volume ii., p. 155.

the quality of legal tender.[1] The Continental Congress not being a regular government, and not having the power to make laws for the regulation of private transactions, referred the matter to the State legislatures."

This brings us to a consideration of the theory of legal tender under our present Constitution. Has the Congress of the United States the power to make bills of credit a legal tender? The Constitution, as adopted by the Constitutional Convention, is silent on this point. But this question had the serious consideration of the Constitutional Convention. The original draft of the Constitution, as reported by the Committee on Detail, gave to Congress the power "to borrow money, and emit bills on the credit of the United States." But ten days later the convention eliminated the words "emit bills" by a vote of nine to two states, only New Jersey and Maryland being in favor of retaining this phrase.[2] The proceedings of the Convention touching this point are interesting in the light of the present attitude of the Supreme Court upon the question. There can be no doubt that if the Convention were opposed to expressly giving to Congress the power to emit bills of credit, it would have been far from their desire to allow them, if issued under some implied power of Congress, to be made legal tender for the payment

[1] Bancroft's *History*, volume vii., p. 324.
[2] See Madison's *Journal of the Federal Convention* (Scott's Edition), pp. 454, 543.

of private debts. The Convention did take the precaution to deny the power to the states of emitting bills of credit.[1]

This limitation upon the power of the several states had ample justification. Mr. Justice Martin, in the Metropolitan Bank v. Van Dyck,[2] justifies the wisdom of the Convention upon this point in the following language:

"Considering the subject or object of these powers, and the circumstance that the people were members of other bodies politic possessing certain powers in common with all independent states, which powers, if exercised by them, would embarrass, derange, and might effectually destroy the common system established by the Federal Government, it was absolutely necessary to impose certain prohibitions upon these other bodies politic —the States. Among these prohibitions, I have always regarded (so far as the peace of the States and the harmony of the system are concerned) those which prohibit the States from making anything but gold or silver coin a tender for the payment of debts, and from passing any law impairing the obligation of contracts, as of supreme importance. If these powers had been suffered to remain with the States, it is quite obvious that difficulty between the people of different States would soon have arisen, endangering peace and harmony between them. Distrust would have existed, and there would have been an absence of that confidence necessary as a base for commercial and other intercourse between

[1] See Constitution, Article I., Section X.
[2] 27 New York, 515; also The Federalist Papers, No. XLIII.

them. Independent nations may protect their merchants and citizens from the frauds of other nations consequent upon a debasement of the coin or a change of the measure of value in which debts are to be paid (or the depreciation of a national paper currency) or for a neglect or refusal to pay, by a resort to war. But the States have no right or power to make war upon each other, and they are prohibited from doing certain things which might be a just cause of war; and the people have entrusted the regulation of these subjects to a general common government."

The wisdom of denying to the states the right of issuing bills of credit was recognized by the states, and very generally accepted without protest. The only question that arose was as to *what constituted a bill of credit* in the constitutional sense. This question was answered in the decision of the Supreme Court in the cases of Craig *v.* Missouri[1] and Briscoe *v.* Bank of Kentucky.[2] In the former case the Court said that "to constitute a bill of credit within the Constitution it must be issued by a State, and be designed to circulate as money." A more difficult question arose in the case of Darrington *v.* Missouri[3] in which the Supreme Court, speaking through Chief Justice Marshall, applied this constitutional restriction of the states to certain loan certificates. The statute under review was "An act for the establishment of loan offices," which attempted to compel certain certificates to be accepted "at the treasury

[1] 11 Peters, 257.   [2] 4 Peters, 410.   [3] 13 Howard, 12.

of any loan office in the State of Missouri in discharge of taxes or debts due the State." Justice Marshall in this case defined "bills of credit" as "a paper medium intended to circulate between individuals and between government and individuals for the ordinary purposes of society." After carefully reviewing the history of these bills and showing their mischievous effects, he classed them as bills of credit, and declared the sections of the law relating to these certificates unconstitutional. This decision was rendered at the January term of the Court in 1830. The broad application here given to the restriction had the effect of giving full effect to the constitutional provision without further question on the part of the states. The more complicated question of the power of the Federal Government to emit such bills and to make them legal tender was not to be answered until more than a generation later.

With the beginning of the Civil War and the problem of securing revenue with which to maintain an armed force, Congress was compelled to resort to an indirect credit system, which would have hardly been resorted to in times of peace. Under the power to borrow money, Congress provided for the issue of treasury notes designed to circulate as money. Under the established doctrine of implied powers, this power could not be questioned; but Congress went further and made these notes legal tender for the payment of all debts due to the United States, and, also, for the discharge of all private debts. To make these notes legal tender for debts due the United States had already been recognized, but to make them legal tender in payment of debts of a private nature was new and a power upon which issue was to be joined.

While few questioned the power of Congress to issue paper money, many opposed such an act on economic grounds. This opposition had manifested itself as a corollary to the opposition to the United States Bank at an earlier date. In 1836, the Democratic platform, upon which Martin Van Buren was elected, declared "hostility to bank notes and paper money as a circulating medium." The Republican platform of 1864 made the Legal Tender Act a real issue by declaring "that it is the duty of every loyal State to sustain the credit and to promote the use of the national currency." Under normal conditions this would have resulted in making the Legal Tender Act the paramount issue before the people.

The soundness of the act was very generally questioned, which had the effect of bringing it before the courts, and at a very early date after its enactment, before the Supreme Court. The earliest cases[1] grew out of the refusal to accept tenders in currency when gold or silver were specified in the contracts. It was uniformly held that such tenders were insufficient because the

[1] Bronson v. Rodes, 7 Wallace, 229; Butler v. Harwitz, 7 Wallace, 256; Bronson v. Kimpton, 8 Wallace, 444.

terms of the contract had not been complied with. None of these cases went into the constitutionality of the act.

The constitutionality of the Legal Tender Act of 1862 came before the Supreme Court for consideration in the case of Hepburn v. Griswold,[1] and the decision was handed down February 7, 1870. Chief Justice Chase, who rendered the decision, held the act unconstitutional. The Court determined the issue upon the question as to the limitation of the implied powers of Congress. The principle laid down in M'Cullough v. the State of Maryland was used as a text. "Let the end be legitimate, let it be within the scope of the Constitution, and all means which are appropriate, which are plainly adapted to that end, which are not prohibited, but consistent with the spirit and letter of the Constitution, are constitutional." The Chief Justice then contrasts "appropriate" acts with those which might in a vague, indefinite way promote an object within Congressional power. To stretch the Constitution to cover the latter under the doctrine of implied power, he contends, would result in both confusion and danger.

" It would convert the Government, which the people ordained as a Government of limited powers, into a Government of unlimited powers. It would confuse the boundaries which separate the executive and judicial from the legislative

[1] 8 Wallace, 513.

authority. It would obliterate every criterion which this Court, speaking through the venerated Chief Justice in the case already cited, has established for the determination of the question whether legislative acts are constitutional or unconstitutional. We are unable to persuade ourselves that an expedient of this sort is an appropriate and plainly adapted means for the execution of the power to declare and carry on war. If it adds nothing to the utility of the notes, it cannot be upheld as a means to the end in furtherance of which the notes are issued. Nor can it, in our judgment, be upheld as such, if, while facilitating in some degree the circulation of the notes, it debases and injures the currency in its proper use to a much greater degree.

" But there is another view which seems to us decisive, to whatever expressed power the supposed implied power in question may be referred. In the rule stated by Chief Justice Marshall, the words appropriate, plainly adapted, really calculated, are qualified by the limitations that the means must be not prohibited, but consistent with the letter and spirit of the Constitution. Nothing so prohibited or inconsistent can be regarded as appropriate, or plainly adapted, or really calculated means to any end.

" Let us inquire then, first, whether making bills of credit a legal tender to the extent indicated is consistent with the spirit of the Constitution. Among the great cardinal principles of that instrument no one is more conspicuous or more venerable than the establishment of justice. And what was intended by the establishment of justice in the minds of the people who ordained it, is, happily, not a matter of disputation. It is not left to inference or conjecture, especially in its relations to contracts. It is then argued that, although there is no expressed prohibition on the United States, as there is on the States, to pass laws impairing the obligation of contracts, still by the general force and tenor of the Constitution they are prohibited from passing any such laws, except such as only impair them incidentally. The Legal Tender Act is held to impair the obligation of contracts and also to be in violation of the Fifth Amendment, which provides that, 'No person shall be deprived of life, liberty, or property without due process of law, nor shall private property be taken for public use without just compensation.'"

The Court concludes as follows:

"To uphold this doctrine would carry the doctrine of implied powers very far beyond any extent hitherto given to it. It asserts that whatever in any degree promotes an end within the scope of a general power, whether, in the correct sense of the word, appropriate or not, may be done in the exercise of an implied power. We are obliged to conclude that an act making mere promises to pay dollars a legal tender in payment of debts previously contracted, is not a means appropriate, plainly adapted, really calculated to carry into effect any express power vested in Congress; that such an act is inconsistent with the spirit of the Constitution; and that it is prohibited by the Constitution."

The effect of this decision was to arouse widespread interest in the question, and to draw more intensely the party lines with reference to it. The Republican party disagreed with reference to this issue. In the Republican platform of 1872, two years after this decision, and upon which Grant ran and was elected President, the boast was made that "a uniform national currency has been provided, and repudiation frowned down"; while the Liberal Republican platform, with Horace Greeley as the advocate, favored a "speedy return to specie payment as demanded alike by the highest consideration of commercial morality and honest government." Had Webster been living at this time, he would doubtless have been in accord with the Greeley wing of the Republican party, for, said he, "We have suffered more from this cause" (referring to the issue of paper money) "than from every other cause or calamity. It has killed more men, pervaded and corrupted the choicest interests of our country more, and done more injustice, than even the arms and artifices of our enemy." The Democratic platform of 1872 was silent on this subject, but four years later, in the famous platform upon which Samuel J. Tilden ran for the Presidency, it declared, "Reform is necessary to establish a sound currency, restore the public credit, and to maintain the national honor." This was the attitude of the leading parties during the time the famous Legal Tender cases were being adjudicated by the Supreme Court.

At the time the decision was rendered in Hepburn *v.* Griswold, two vacancies existed in the Supreme Court. The events connected with these appointments have furnished much cause for criticism of the President and his administration at this time. The number of Supreme Court justices was changed by statute three times between 1863 and 1869. An act of March 3, 1863, changed the number of justices of the Court from nine to ten members. By the provisions of an act of July 23, 1866, it was enacted "that no vacancy in the office of Associate Justice should be filled by appointment until the number of Associates should be reduced to six, and thereafter the Supreme Court should consist of a Chief Justice and six Associate Justices." By an act of April 10, 1869, the number was again changed, this time to a Chief Justice and eight Associate Justices. The provision of this act and the resignation of Justice Grier were the causes of the two vacancies at the time of the decision in Hepburn v. Griswold. These various acts had the effect of causing many people to believe that politics was the controlling motive behind these measures, and when President Grant appointed Mr. Justice Strong and Mr. Justice Bradley to the Supreme Bench, both of whom voted to reverse the decision in Hepburn v. Griswold, not only the Democrats, but many Republicans, openly censured the President, and for a time his reëlection was in serious doubt.

With this increased number, the same question came before the Court in the cases of Knox v. Lee and Parker v. Davis.[1] These cases are notable because of the scholarly briefs submitted by

[1] 12 Wallace, 287.

learned counsel, the very able opinion rendered by
Justice Strong, the elaborate and emphatic opinion of Justice Bradley, whom Senator Hoar said
"the general voice of the profession and of his
brethren of the bench would place at the head of
all living jurists," and the legal learning displayed
in the dissenting opinions of Justices Chase,
Clifford, and Field. The two controlling questions
before the Court were, "are the acts of Congress
known as the Legal Tender Acts constitutional
when applied to contracts made before their
passage; and secondly, are they valid as applicable
to debts contracted since their enactment?"

In reversing the decision in Hepburn *v.* Griswold,
the Court argued along the line of expediency,
and public necessity, and vaguely hinted at such a
power of Congress resulting from existing war
and public danger.

"It would be difficult [said the Court] to over-
estimate the consequences which must follow our
decision. They will affect the entire business
of the country, and take hold of the possible
continued existence of the Government. If it be
held by this Court that Congress has no constitutional power under any circumstances, or in any
emergency, to make treasury notes a legal tender
for the payment of all debts (a power confessedly
possessed by every independent sovereignty other
than the United States), the Government is without the means of self-preservation, which, all
must admit, may, in certain contingencies, become
indispensable, even if they were not when the

acts of Congress now called into question were enacted."

The Court here seems to justify the Legal Tender Act as a means of preserving the Union. This line of argument is followed by a discussion of the consequences to the commercial interests, contending that to annul the act would make of the Government an instrument of injustice.

"If, now, by our decision, it be established that these debts and obligations can be discharged only by gold coin; if, contrary to the expectations of all parties to these contracts, legal tender notes are rendered unavailable, the Government has become an instrument of the grossest injustice; all debtors loaded with an obligation it was never contemplated they should assume, a large percentage is added to every debt, and such must become the demand for gold to satisfy contracts that ruinous sacrifices, general distress, and bankruptcy may be expected. These consequences are too obvious to admit of question."

It can hardly be said that up to this point the argument was a strictly legal one, and, in fact, about the only legal argument used was expressed in the following language:

"There is no well-defined distinction to be made between the constitutional validity of an act of Congress declaring treasury notes a legal tender for the payment of debts contracted after passage and that of an act making them a legal tender for the discharge of all debts, as well those incurred before as those made after its enactment. There may be a difference in the effects produced by the acts, and the hardship of their operation, but in both cases the fundamental question, that which tests the validity of the legislation, is, can Congress constitutionally give to treasury notes the character and quality of money? Can such notes be constituted a legitimate circulating medium, having a defined legal value?

The Court then proceeds to answer this question upon the ground of the implied powers in the affirmative. The decision concludes with an allusion to the decision which it reversed.

"We are not aware of anything else which has been advanced in support of the proposition that the Legal Tender Acts were forbidden by either the letter or spirit of the Constitution. If, therefore, they were, what we have endeavored to show, appropriate means for legitimate ends, they were not transgressive of the authority vested in Congress.

"But without extending our remarks further, it will be seen that we hold the acts of Congress constitutional, as applied to contracts made either before or after their passage."

It was not until 1884 that this question was finally disposed of. This time the case was that of Julliard v. Greenman.[1] The interest that attaches to this case is due largely to the fact that it was the only one of the Legal Tender cases that was decided upon strictly legal reasoning. The deci-

[1] 110 United States, 421.

sion is of interest, also, because of the fact that it was decided on much broader ground than the former decisions, there being no attempt made to justify these acts upon the grounds of national self-preservation or commercial necessity. The concluding paragraphs illustrate the line of argument used.

"Congress, as the legislature of a sovereign nation, being expressly empowered by the Constitution to 'lay and collect taxes, to pay the debts and provide for the common defense and general welfare of the United States,' to 'borrow money on the credit of the United States,' and 'to coin money and regulate the value thereof and of foreign coin,' and being clearly authorized, as incidental to the exercise of these great powers, to emit bills of credit, to charter national banks, and to provide a national currency for the whole people, in the form of coin, treasury notes, and national bank bills; and the power to make notes of the Government a legal tender payment of private debts being one of the powers belonging to the sovereignty in other civilized nations, and not expressly withheld from Congress by the Constitution; we are irresistibly impelled to the conclusion that the impressing upon the treasury notes of the United States the quality of being a legal tender in payment of private debts is an appropriate means, conducive and plainly adapted to the execution of the undoubted powers of Congress, consistent with the letter and the spirit of the Constitution, and therefore, within the meaning of that instrument, necessary and proper for carrying into execution the powers vested by this

11

Constitution in the Government of the United States.

"Such being our conclusion in matter of law, the question whether at any particular time, in war or in peace, the exigency is such, by reason of unusual and pressing demands on the resources of the Government, or of the inadequacy of the supply of gold and silver coin to furnish the currency needed for the use of the Government and of the people, that it is, as matter of fact, wise and expedient to resort to this means, is a political question, to be determined by Congress, when the question to be afterward passed upon by the courts. To quote once more from the judgment in M'Cullough v. Maryland: 'Where the law is not prohibited, and is really calculated to effect any one of the objects intrusted to the Government, to undertake here to inquire into the degree of its necessity would be to pass the line which circumscribes the judicial department and to tread on legislative ground.'[1]

"It follows that the act of May the 31st, 1878, c. 146, is constitutional and valid; and that the circuit court rightly held that in treasury notes reissued and kept in circulation, under that act, tender of lawful money in payment of the defendant's debt was a debt due to the plaintiff."

In spite of the fact that this decision closely followed the reasoning of Chief Justice Marshall in M'Cullough v. Maryland, and closely adhered to the implied powers under those provisions of the Constitution to which these powers had been applied, still the decision evoked much adverse

[1] 4 Wheaton, 423.

criticism. *The Financial Chronicle*, in commenting on the decision, said: "All reliance upon the constitutional inhibition to do anything with the currency which Congress may have a whim to do must be abandoned henceforth and forever."

E. Benjamin Andrews[1] says in commenting upon the Legal Tender cases that,

"An enactment by Congress the Supreme Court presumes to be constitutional unless it is certainly unconstitutional. If there is doubt upon the point there is no doubt. Congress is right. The authority to 'emit bills of credit' as legal tender was not expressly delegated to the Federal Government, but it may well claim place in the goodly families of 'implied powers,' apparently being implied by its prohibitions upon the States, or involved in the power to borrow money, or in that to regulate commerce. Again, if Congress could pass such a law to meet an exigency, as held in Parker *v.* Davis, Congress must be left to determine when the exigency exists. The intention of the Fathers to inhibit bills of credit cannot be conclusively shown. Even if it were certain it would be inconclusive; the question being not what they intended to do, but what they actually did in framing the Constitution.

"The wisdom of the legal tender law is a different question, but, like the other, should not be pronounced upon without reflection. It was easy to condemn it after the event."

At any event it proved one of the most perplexing

[1] See Hawthorne-Schouler-Andrews, *History of United States*, vol. viii., p. 225.

problems that the Supreme Court was ever called upon to solve. This is evidenced by the fact that from first to last the Supreme Court decided the question in three different ways, a fact that is unique in the decisions of this tribunal. But in the diversity of opinion that existed in the Court, it can be clearly seen that an honest attempt was being made to reconcile the commercial and political interests of the country with the organic law of the land.

CHAPTER VIII

THEORY OF A PROTECTIVE TARIFF

NO single issue has persisted so long, or proved of so great historic consequence to our country as that of a protective tariff. It was one of the first matters under debate in the First Congress of the United States in 1789; it has been a persistent matter for consideration in many Congresses; it was the leading issue in the political campaign of 1912, and the effects of the recent tariff revision by the Democratic Congress and the President's approval will largely determine the results of the next presidential election. The second act that Washington signed was a tariff act. It was signed on July the fourth, 1789, and it has, on account of this fact, been called by its friends, "The Second Declaration of Independence." The act provided for a tariff on rum, molasses (which was principally used for rum-making), steel, coal, etc. James Madison was the author of the original measure. The first decided opposition to the bill came from South Carolina in opposing the tax on tallow candles. The clashing of commercial interests brought forth angry debate. Both protection and free trade marshaled their forces in the First Congress, and these forces have continued to be arrayed against each other through the century and a quarter of our history.

Madison's[1] bill was the result of a memorial sent to Congress by the merchants and manufacturers of Baltimore. This address presented conditions in the following language:

"Since the close of the late war, and the completion of the Revolution, they have observed with serious regrets the manufacturing and trading interests of the country rapidly declining, and the attempts of the State legislatures to remedy the evil failing of their object; that, in the present melancholy state of our country, the number of poor increasing for want of employment, foreign debts accumulating, houses and lands depreciating in value, and trade and manufactures languishing and expiring, they look up to the Supreme Legislature of the United States as the guardian of the whole empire, and from their united wisdom and patriotism, and ardent love of their country, expect to derive that aid and assistance which alone can dissipate their just apprehensions, and animate them with hopes of success in the future, by imposing on all foreign articles, which can be made in America, such duties as will give a just and decided preference to their labors; discountenancing that trade which tends so materially to injure them and impoverish their country; meas-

[1] Madison claimed to believe in the principle of free trade, but admitted the necessity of protection in time of war, and for the encouragement of infant industries.—See his *Works*, vol. iii., p. 42.

ures which, in their consequences, may also contribute to the discharge of the national debt and the due support of the Government."

This memorial clearly lays the premise for a protective tariff. Its defenders saw hope for the languishing and expiring manufactures in imposing duties on "all foreign articles which can be manufactured in this country." It is not clear what position Madison occupied as to protection. His measure was, doubtless, intended as a revenue measure only, but he refused to define his position on the subject. It developed that the manufacturing states of Massachusetts, New York, Pennsylvania, and Connecticut seized upon the principle of "protection for our infant industries" as the solution to their commercial difficulties. As self-interest fostered the doctrine in the manufacturing states, so the same spirit caused violent opposition to it in the non-manufacturing states. No other question in our political history, except that of slavery, has been so completely influenced by physiographical conditions.

The opponents of the protective principle questioned the soundness of this kind of legislation on constitutional grounds, this argument being the basis of attack in 1789 and 1816, and more earnestly resorted to in the famous tariff debates of 1824. Not only Clay, the sponsor of the protective system, but Adams, Crawford, and Jackson were declared to be advocates of this American system. [1]

[1] See Taussig's *Tariff History of the United States*, p. 74.

Clay, in his early Congressional career as a United States Senator (1809–1811), strongly supported the protective principle on the ground of the established rule of loose construction. "The nation," he says, "which imports its clothing from abroad is but little less dependent than if it imported its bread." This statement seems to seek to justify the principle on the ground of expediency. He argued along the same line in the debate on the tariff of 1824. But his debates on this subject evidently regard the principle as authorized under the provision of the Constitution that gives Congress power to lay taxes, duties, imposts, and excises. Pomeroy says[1] on this point:

"The partisans of a strict construction have urged that the levying of duties must be confined to so much as may be necessary for a tax. But during a large portion of our history a tariff has been in operation which was designed, and did operate, to protect certain home interests. A protective tariff is certainly not indispensable to the execution of the power to levy taxes; but it is as certainly one of the methods of exercising that power."

A compromise view seems to have been held by some. They were what has been called "moderate protectionists," of whom Webster was the leader during the early tariff period. He held that the whole subject was one of expediency; that the

[1] *Constitutional Law* (Bennett's Edition), p. 217.

protective system should be so restricted as not
to destroy commerce.[1]

The tariff of 1828, otherwise known as the "tariff
of abominations," brought out definite sectional
strife. The National Republicans, relying on the
doctrine of loose construction and armed with the
lucid report of Alexander Hamilton, which was
made to Congress in 1791, were able to carry
into law this famous act, against the united
opposition of the strict construction followers of
Jefferson.

Scarcely had the act become law when the
tariff debate went beyond the halls of Congress
to all parts of the country. Five Southern states
(North Carolina, South Carolina, Virginia, Georgia,
and Alabama) protested against the act on the
ground that it was destructive to the interests of
the people of these states. The South, as well as
some other sections of the country, saw in this
tariff measure Congressional support of the commercial interests of the North, at the expense of
the South. This view of the matter precipitated
Nullification.

South Carolina became the storm-center of the
opposition. The agitation formally began in 1821
when McDuffie in a pamphlet opposed the doctrine of State Sovereignty. The question that presented itself was: Who is the judge of the powers
of the Federal Government? Webster replied,
"the Nation"; Calhoun answered that the "state

[1] See Webster's speech in Congress on April 1 and 2, 1828.

is judge on all matters pertaining to itself."[1] This discussion led to the publication of Turnbull's pamphlet, *The Crisis*, which contained the first formulated doctrine of Nullification. This pamphlet was heartily indorsed by Cooper, Calhoun, and Hayne. When the Legislature of South Carolina met in December, 1825, the House adopted the following resolution: "It is an unconstitutional exercise of power on the part of Congress to lay duties to protect domestic manufactures." Resolutions supporting the views of South Carolina were passed by North Carolina, Alabama, and Georgia. To make the situation more acute, several Northern states, principally New York, Pennsylvania, Ohio, and Massachusetts, not only defended the tariff laws, but urged an increase of the import duties. In addition to this, late in 1831 a Free Trade Convention was held in Philadelphia and a Protective Convention in New York City.

In July, 1832, Congress revised the tariff of 1828, but left it decidedly protective. Immediately the members of Congress from South Carolina notified their people at home that "protection had become the settled policy of the Nation and all hope for relief had irrevocably passed." In November, 1832, in convention assembled at Columbia, South Carolina formally adopted the famous Ordinance of Nullification. The protective doc-

[1] See on this point Fess' *History of Political Theory and Party Organization in the United States*, pp. 154 and 155.

trine had, after forty years of agitation, wrought its deadly work.

On December 12, 1831, six months preceding the tariff revision of 1832, the Whigs or National-Republicans in their first formal platform announced the doctrine, to which their successor, the Republican party of to-day, has adhered, that "an adequate protection to American industry is indispensable to the prosperity of the country; and an abandonment of the policy at this period would be attended with consequences ruinous to the best interests of the Nation." Clay was nominated on this platform in recognition of his loyalty and prominence as an advocate of the protective theory. For the first time, the Democratic party also held a national convention and renominated Jackson. This campaign turned to the bank as an issue, rather than to that of the tariff, for the Compromise Tariff Act was passed in 1833, which remained in force for nine years. There is little doubt that this act was the result of an agreement between Clay, the representative of the protectionists, and Calhoun, the leader of the advocates of free trade. The effect of this measure was to postpone the tariff as an issue for a time.

In 1863, the Democrats of New York adopted a declaration which was regarded as the sentiment of the party throughout the country, although the party in convention did not formally adopt a platform. The language used in the New York declaration was as follows: "We declare unqualified hostility to any and all monopolies by legislation because they are violations of equal rights of the people; hostility to the dangerous and unconstitutional creation of vested rights and prerogatives by legislation, because they are usurpations of the people's sovereignty." In substance this general sentiment was expressed in a number of the Democratic platforms that followed. The first strong and positive declaration of the party against the theory of protection was announced in the platform of 1876, in the convention which nominated Tilden. It said:

"We denounce the present tariff, levied upon nearly 4000 articles, as a masterpiece of injustice, inequality, and false pretense. It yields a dwindling, not a yearly rising revenue. It has impoverished many industries to subsidize a few. It prohibits imports that might purchase the products of American labor. It has degraded American commerce from the first to an inferior rank on the high seas. It has cut down the sales of American manufactures at home and abroad, and depleted the returns of American agriculture—an industry followed by half of our people."

Four years later the party came out "for a tariff for revenue only." In opposition to this teaching of the Democratic party the modern Republican party has taken firmer ground in recent years for the principle of protection. For instance, their platform of 1888 denounced the Mills Bill in the following language:

"We are uncompromisingly in favor of the American system of protection; we protest against its destruction as proposed by the President and his party. They serve the interest of Europe; we will support the interest of America. We accept the issue and confidently appeal to the people for their judgment. The protective system must be maintained. Its abandonment has always been followed by general disaster to all interests, except those of the usurer and the sheriff. We denounce the Mills Bill as destructive to the general business, the labor, and the farming interest of the country."

This view is in harmony with the views held by the Whigs of 1842, who were responsible for the tariff of that year. The Democratic party throughout its history has opposed the principle of protection, while the various parties which have opposed it have taken the side of protection. Each of the leading parties in recent years has placed a tariff plank in its platform. It has been one question that arose with the first breath of our nationality and has persisted throughout our history, increasing in importance as the years come and go. It is a more dominant issue to-day than at any earlier period of our history. The present attitude of the two dominant parties may fairly be inferred from the platforms of 1904. In that year the Democratic platform had this declaration: "We favor a tariff limited to the needs of the Government economically administered, and so levied as not to discriminate against any industry, class, or section, to the end that the burdens of taxation shall be distributed as equally as possible." The Republican party of that year, in their platform, declared that "protection which guards and develops our industries is a cardinal policy of the Republican party. The measure of protection should always at least equal the difference in the cost of production at home and abroad."

The Democratic and Republican platforms of 1908 and 1912 reaffirm in substance these same ideas. The Progressive (Republican) platform of 1912 declared for protection "which shall equalize conditions of competition between the United States and foreign countries, both for the farmer and manufacturer, and which shall maintain for labor an adequate standard of living." This seems to represent a position midway between the uncompromising protective policy of the Republicans and the "tariff for revenue policy" of the Democrats. These are the prevailing viewpoints on the tariff question to-day.

Having briefly traced party attitude on the question, we turn to consider to what extent judicial opinion has favored one or the other of the views upon the question. Those who opposed the doctrine claimed that it was unconstitutional on two propositions: (1) That it was not a necessary means of laying and collecting taxes, and that such a tax was not contemplated by the framers of the Constitution. In other words they based their claim upon the doctrine of strict construction. This view was, as has been shown, very early overthrown by the courts in establishing the doctrine of loose construction. (2) That a protective tariff was unconstitutional because, on account of the diversity of climate and the occupations of the people, it must operate to benefit one section of the country at the expense of another. Strange as it may seem, although the tariff had the effect to involve great commercial interests, this question was never directly involved in a suit at law or in equity. A number of decisions, however, have grown out of the issues, from which · we can infer the judicial mind on the subject.

The earliest case touching upon the subject was that of Hylton v. the United States.[1] This was a case in which an action of debt had been instituted in the name of the United States against Daniel Hylton, to recover the penalty imposed by an act of Congress of the 5th day of June, 1794, for not entering and paying the duty on a number of carriages. Issue was joined on the ground that the tax was a direct tax and, therefore, unconstitutional. The Government was represented by Alexander Hamilton, Secretary of the Treasury, and Attorney-General Lee, who ably contended for the constitutionality of the law. The Court upheld the law, contending that it was not a direct tax, but merely a duty. The legal right to levy a duty was announced in these words:

[1] 3 Dallas, 171.

"Duties, imposts, and excises," said the Court (Justice Chase delivered this opinion), "were enumerated, after the general term, taxes, for the purpose of declaring that they were to be laid by the rule of uniformity. I consider the Constitution to stand in this manner. A general power is given to Congress to lay and collect taxes of every kind or nature, without any restraint, except only on exports, but two rules are prescribed for the Government, namely, uniformity and apportionment. Three kinds of taxes, to wit: duties, imposts, and excises of the first rule, and capitation, or other direct taxes, by the second rule."

Justice Iredell, in concurring with this opinion of the Chief Justice, said: "Congress possesses the power of taxing all taxable objects, without limitation, with the particular exception of a duty on exports." This decision was rendered within one year of the time the tariff law on which it was based became effective. This decision has not been disturbed. It shows the early desire of the Court to uphold the revenue system of the country. It had the effect of making possible the enforcement of the various excise laws through which enormous revenues have been collected by the Government. This decision shows the truth of Cooley's statement that "the power to impose taxes is one so unlimited in force and so searching in extent, that the courts scarcely venture to declare that it is subject to any restrictions whatever, except such as rest in the discretion of the authority which exercises it."[1]

[1] Cooley's *Constitutional Limitations*, p. 587.

A decision somewhat more in point was that of the brig *Aurora*.[1] This decision was handed down on February 26, 1813. An appeal had been taken from the judgment of the District Court for the District of Orleans, which condemned the cargo of the brig *Aurora* for having been imported from Great Britain in violation of the fourth and fifth sections of the Non-Intercourse Act of March 1, 1809. This act was a modification of the Embargo Act, which was repealed three days before Jefferson retired from the presidency. The Non-Intercourse Act allowed our merchantmen to go abroad, but forbade them to trade with either Great Britain or France. Section IV. of this act provided that "after the 20th day of May next, it shall not be lawful to import into the United States or the territories goods, etc., from England," and the fifth section made forfeiture the penalty. The Embargo Act and this partial Embargo Act were the doctrine of protection carried to its logical conclusion. If Congress could put a protective tariff on goods to protect our infant industries, it could prohibit the importation of foreign goods from all countries or from any country in the interest of home manufacturers. The Embargo Act of 1807 never came before the courts, but the Legislature of Massachusetts declared it "unconstitutional and not legally binding."[2] This belief

[1] 7 Cranch, 380.
[2] Adams's *United States History*, vol. iv., McMaster's *U. S.*, vol. iii.

12

on the part of New England produced the Hartford Convention.[1] Many believed that if Congress could pass an Embargo, it could also pass a protective tariff that was so high as to prevent the importation of goods from a foreign country and give to American manufacturing interest a monopoly by law; but when the Non-Intercourse Act came to be passed on in the brig *Aurora* case, the Court seemed not to have questioned the power of Congress to enact the law. Justice Johnson delivered the opinion of the Court and sustained the law and the right of Congress to enforce it after its conditional expiration, either expressly or conditionally as their judgment should direct.

A little later the same sections of this act were sustained in an opinion rendered by Chief Justice Marshall in the case of the schooner *Hoppett*.[2] The unsettled conditions that existed between the United States, England, and France brought the acts referred to into existence, and this may account for the fact that the courts never questioned the power that created them. Certainly no power was given to Congress in time of peace to enact a law that would destroy the commerce and prosperity of any section of the country. The acceptance of the right of Congress to enact these laws really settled the policy of the country. Many later decisions bear interesting testimony of the attitude of the courts upon the subject.

[1] Walker's *Making of the Nation*, p. 200.
[2] Schooner *Hoppett v.* U. S., 7 Cranch, 386.

In 1885, the Supreme Court in an opinion delivered by Justice Matthews said:

"The whole system" (referring to the tariff system), "must be regarded in each alteration, and no disturbance allowed of existing legislative rules of general application beyond the clear intention of Congress. In the interpretation of our revenue laws, this Court has not been disposed to apply with strictness the rule which repeals a prior statute by implication, where a subsequent one has made provision upon the same subject, and differing in some respects from the former, but has been inclined to uphold both, unless the repugnance is so clear and positive as to leave no doubt as to the intent of Congress."[1]

This case shows by implication the effort the Court would make to sustain a tariff law.

An attack was made on the constitutionality of the Tariff Act of 1890, in the case of Marshall Field and Company v. Clark.[2] It was claimed that an attempt was made in this Act to delegate certain powers to the President that were legislative in their nature, rather than executive. While this point is immaterial to this discussion, the Court used this language, which is in point:

"Unless it be impossible," said Justice Harlan, "to avoid it, a general revenue statute should never be declared inoperative in all its parts because a particular part relating to a distinct

[1] Saxonville Mills v. Russell.   [2] 143 U. S., 649.

subject may be invalid. A different rule might be disastrous to the financial operations of the Government, and produce the utmost confusion in the business of the country."

Chief Justice Fuller thought the particular section unconstitutional but agreed with the majority of the Court in the conclusions reached. He said: "Whilst, however, we cannot agree to the proposition that the particular section is valid and constitutional, we do not regard it as such an essential part of the Tariff Act as to invalidate all the other sections." The Court, however, in this decision did not fail to reveal the fact that they were of the opinion that that provision of the McKinley tariff that placed a bounty on sugar was unconstitutional. "A tax laid for neither the object of paying the debts nor providing for the common defense nor general welfare of the United States is unconstitutional as an excess of legislative power." It seems to have been the studious intention of the Federal courts to associate tariff with a tax. Bascom[1] accounts for the courts sustaining the tariff laws throughout our history on these grounds: "The protective policy of the United States was instituted so early, grew by such insensible degrees, and was so closely associated with taxation, that the question of its constitutional right was blurred."

This idea was a prominent feature of the Head

[1] *Growth of Nationality in the United States*, p. 35.

Money cases.   In Arnold *v.* United States[1] the Court says,

"The idea that runs from the very first Congress down to the present date, in laying duties, imposts, and excises, the rule of inherent uniformity, or in other words, intrinsically equal and uniform taxes, has been disregarded, and the principle of geographical uniformity consistently enforced."

There have been a few exceptions, however, to the attempt of the courts to identify a tariff with a tax. For instance, in Arnold *v.* United States[2] the Court says, "The idea that runs through the Tariff Act of 1890 is that of protection to our manufactures." A tariff could hardly be justified on broader grounds than this.

The tariff principle has been held to apply to our recent Spanish acquisitions. The Island of Porto Rico, after its cession to the United States by the treaty with Spain, which was proclaimed at Washington on April 11, 1899, though it had not been formerly embraced by Congress within the customs' unions of the states, was no longer foreign territory within the meaning of the Dingley Tariff Act of July 24, 1897.[3] A similar decision was made in the Diamong Ring case with reference to the Philippine Islands.

In conclusion we can hardly explain the causes

[1] 112 U. S., 580.   [2] 147 U. S., 494.
[3] De Lima *v.* Bidwell, 182 U. S. 1.

and status of the tariff question better than in the words of John Bascom,[1] who says:

"A written constitution has this distinct evil—that it gives occasion to technical discussions as to whether a given power is contained in the original grant, and these discussions obscure the more important question whether the given power, if present, can be advantageously exercised. The formal inquiry crowds out the substantial one of the wisdom of the proposed policy. This has been illustrated in discussions of the doctrine of protection. An effort was early made to disprove the right of Congress to impose protective duties. The power conceded to Congress to lay taxes is so broad, and the power to lay discriminating duties has been so wrapped up in this power, that the effort to prove its unconstitutionality has failed and has been abandoned, with the exception of here and there a doctrinaire. The question whether Congress might wisely impose protective duties has received less thorough consideration because of the victory gained as to the power to impose them. It is a familiar weakness in human affairs that the power to do a given thing operates as a motive to do it. Again and again in our history the familiar right and necessity of taxation have hidden from sight some vital policy not necessarily associated with them."

With the recent support given the doctrine of protection by the courts, the dominant parties have both assumed an advanced position on the subject. Before the tariff period from 1887 to

[1] *Growth of Nationality in the United States*, p. 34.

1900, which saw the debate and the enactment of the McKinley Tariff Act, the Republican party advocated a protective tariff as a temporary policy. As President Garfield said: "They were for a protective tariff that leads ultimately to free trade." This view has been abandoned by the Republicans and they have substituted for it a permanent policy of protection. On the other hand, the Democrats have moved up from a policy of opposition to all forms of protection to that of a moderate duty or protection to supply the necessary revenue to support the Government. The two leading parties are likely to disagree in the future more in working out the details of the system than in any difference as to policy or principle.

CHAPTER IX

THEORY OF AN INCOME TAX

THE suggestion of an income tax is the result of an attempt to put into effect a low tariff without producing a deficit in the national treasury for the necessary expenses of the Federal Government. It is, therefore, closely related to the tariff as an issue, and has had the support of that party which has favored a low tariff and opposed all forms of protection by governmental agency. The income tax of 1894 was incorporated into the Wilson Tariff Act, which was a Democratic measure, and greatly reduced the existing tariff schedules. The Democratic platform of 1892 was silent upon the subject of an income tax, but the party had promised to revise the tariff downward, and asserted that "the Federal Government has no constitutional power to impose and collect tariff duties, except for the purposes of revenue only," and denounced the McKinley tariff as class legislation. The Republicans did not mention an income tax in their platform, but strongly defended the doctrine of protection. However, the National People's party of that year did declare in favor of a graduated income tax. This was the only sense in which it became an issue in the campaign of 1892. But this was sufficient to call the attention of the country to it, and when the Democrats in Congress gave it their support, it was violently opposed by the Republicans.

Though Cleveland was elected with the reduction of the tariff as the chief issue, when he was inaugurated on March 4, 1893, conditions were such as to make it difficult for the party in power to conform to its platform assertions. At that time the country was on the verge of a panic. The treasury was in a financial strait. The gold supply was so reduced that there was fear that the holders of paper money would make a run on the treasury. The panic was only averted by the support of the banks and the refusal of the Government to purchase more silver. In the face of this the expenses of the Government had greatly increased, and in spite of this fact the Democrats were committed to a policy of tariff reduction. The party sought the solution of this difficult situation in the passage of an income tax of two per cent. on all incomes in excess of four thousand dollars.

The constitutionality of an income tax seems not to have been seriously questioned when the law of 1890 was under consideration by Congress. An income tax had been repeatedly imposed and had been recognized in judicial action. Five acts involving this principle had been passed by Congress before 1860. In the special session of Congress which convened on July 4, 1861, a tax on incomes was passed to assist in defraying the expenses due to the war. Between 1861 and 1870 nine acts were passed involving the income tax principle.[1]

The question of the constitutionality of this kind of tax grew out of the sense in which "direct taxes" was used in the Constitution. The Constitution bestows unlimited power of taxation on the National Government, with one exception and two restrictions. The exception is that of a tax on exports, and the restrictions are (1) uniformity and (2) apportionment.

Our courts have, throughout the history of the country, restricted the meaning of "direct taxes" as used in our Constitution. In this tendency, as in many others, we have been largely influenced by England. Mill[2] says:

"In England there is a popular feeling of old standing, in favor of indirect, or it should be rather said in opposition to direct, taxation. The unpopularity of direct taxation, contrasted with the easy manner in which the public consent to let themselves be fleeced in the prices of commodities, has generated in many friends of improvement a directly opposite mode of thinking to the foregoing. They contend that the very reason which makes direct taxation disagreeable, makes it preferable. Under it, every one knows how much he really pays; and if he votes for a war, or any other expensive national luxury, he does so with his

[1] See Dewey's *Financial History of the United States*, pp. 11, 277, and 305.　　　[2] *Political Economy*, vol. ii., p. 367.

eyes open to what it costs him. If all taxes were direct, taxes would be much more perceived than at present; and there would be a security which now there is not, for economy in the public expenditure."

We have experienced exactly a similar condition in this country. Our legal authorities have been disposed to uphold the principle of indirect taxation, while at the same time the people have been drifting toward a more extended use and meaning of direct taxation, and for the same reasons referred to by Mill.

The tendency of the courts was illustrated in the early case of Hylton v. United States. This case grew out of the refusal to pay a tax which was assessed on pleasure carriages. The payment of the tax was refused, and the fact relied on in the argument of the case was that the tax was direct in its nature and not laid as required by the Constitution. But the Supreme Court refused to class this tax as direct, and held that it was in the form of a duty. This decision was rendered in 1795, and it is significant that three of the judges that rendered the majority opinion were members of the Constitutional Convention.

In the case of Insurance v. Soule[1] the question was raised as to the legality of a tax on the receipts from premiums and assessments. In a unanimous opinion the Court held this not to be a direct tax. Chief Justice Chase reached a similar conclusion

[1] 7 Wallace, 433.

in rendering the opinion in the case of Bank v. Fenno.[1]

But the most important decision on this subject, rendered before the passage of the Act of 1894, was that of Springer v. United States[2] which was rendered in January, 1881. This was an action of ejectment brought by the defendant in error to prevent the sale of certain lots by the collector of taxes in payment of an income tax as provided by an act of Congress passed in 1862. Justice Swain delivered the opinion of the Court, and held that the tax was not a direct tax and therefore a legal tax. He cites a number of authorities to show that direct taxes under the Constitution are restricted to capitation taxes and taxes on real estate, and that this income tax was in the nature of an excise duty. The Court says (in answer to numerous questions and citations raised and quoted in the brief of the plaintiff in error) that "what is a direct tax, is one exclusive in American jurisprudence." The Court, in refusing to accept the definition of direct taxation as used by Mill in his *Political Economy* and Smith in *The Wealth of Nations*, say that all text writers in this country are in entire accord in limiting the meaning of direct taxes to a poll and a land tax.

This was the status of the income tax doctrine at the time of the passage of the income tax law of 1894. Under the dignified doctrine of *stare decisis* no question seemed more completely settled.

[1] 8 Wallace, 533. [2] 102 U. S., 586.

Certainly judicial opinion justified the belief of the people generally, as well as many learned lawyers, that the law, when tested in the courts, would be held valid.

The constitutionality of the act was brought before the courts for consideration in the case of Pollock *v.* Farmers' Loan and Trust Company.[1] The briefs, arguments of learned counsel, and the majority and dissenting opinions of the Court, make this one of the longest reported cases ever decided by the Supreme Court of the United States. The importance of the decision, and the interest that the issue had aroused, attracted the attention of the entire country.

The law was attacked in the briefs and arguments on three grounds: (1) That the tax was direct and did not operate uniformly; (2) it was not apportioned; (3) it attempted to tax the income derived from public or Government bonds. There could not be much question on the last point, for the courts had repeatedly held that the agencies of Government could not be taxed.

Chief Justice Fuller rendered the decision in the case. The student may conveniently divide the opinion into two parts: (1) The judicial and political history of the income tax before the Civil War and (2) the views held by writers subsequent to that period. After citing many authorities the Chief Justice drew the following conclusions

[1] 157 United States, 759.

from judicial dicta and political opinion before the war:

1. That the distinction between direct and indirect taxation was well understood by the framers of the Constitution.

2. That under state systems of taxation all taxes on real estate or personal property or rents or incomes were regarded as direct taxes.

3. That rules of apportionment and uniformity were adopted in view of that distinction and in view of those systems.

4. That whether a tax on carriages was a direct or indirect tax was disputed, but was upheld as an excise duty.

5. That the original expectation was that the power of direct taxation would be seldom exercised.

In beginning the review of the cases cited by counsel in support of the law that have arisen since the Civil War, the Court sought evasion by citing the doctrine of *stare decisis* as follows: "The doctrine of *stare decisis* is a salutary one, and to be adhered to on all proper occasions, but it only arises in respect of decisions directly upon the point in issue." With this remark the Court brushes aside all the legal dicta bearing on the subject.

Then entering upon the merits of the case the Chief Justice contends that a tax on the income of land is the same as a tax on the land, and since a land tax is admitted to be direct, it follows that the income from land is direct.

"The real question is, is there any basis upon which to rest the contention that real estate belongs to one of the great classes of taxes, and the rent or income which is the incident of its ownership belongs to another? We are unable to perceive any ground for the alleged distinction.

"We are of the opinion that the law in question, so far as it levies a tax on the rents or income of real estate, is in violation of the Constitution, and is invalid."

This was the strongest and clearest point made by the Court. The Court's argument that the income tax section of the statute was repugnant to the Constitution because it failed to secure uniformity in its application is evasive and unsatisfactory.

The animus, too, of the Court was revealed, when in the conclusion of the opinion, the declaration was made that upon each of the following questions argued at bar, to wit: 1. Whether the void provisions as to rents and income from real estate invalidated the whole act? 2. Whether as to income from personal property as such, the act is unconstitutional, as laying direct taxes? 3. Whether any part of the tax, if not considered as a direct tax, is invalid for want of uniformity on any of the grounds suggested?—the justices, who heard the argument were equally divided, and, therefore no opinion was expressed.

The effect of this decision was to nullify the law without passing upon the constitutionality of an income tax law. The decision was a disappointment to many, because the constitutionality of such a law had been called into question, and the country at large was in doubt concerning the power of Congress with reference to it. The question was squarely before the Supreme Court, and the fact that the question was evaded looked to many as an attempt to nullify the act without assuming responsibility for declaring the doctrine on which it was based unconstitutional.

However, this case was re-argued in May, 1895, and on May 20, 1895, the Court handed down its opinion, which declared the income tax feature (sections twenty-seven to thirty-seven, inclusive, of the Act of 1894) unconstitutional, and void because *not apportioned according to representation*. Four justices rendered dissenting opinions, among these being a strong opinion by Justice Harlan. The close decision and the importance of the issue left the question in doubt in the minds of many lawyers and other public men.

Some contend that no income tax bill could be drawn that would not be so involved in direct taxation as to make it violate a fundamental principle of our organic law, while others still believed that a bill could be so worded as to overcome the objections of the Supreme Court, and accomplish the desired object. The former view is held by Skinner in his *Issues of American Politics.*[1] He classes taxes under the provisions of the constitution as follows:

[1] Chapter iii., pp. 472 and 483.

I. Direct.
    (1)   Real, viz.: Taxes on Land.
    (2)   Personal, viz.: Income Taxes.
    (3)   Individual, viz.: Capitation Taxes.
II. Indirect.
    Indirect taxes are all personal, viz.: Taxes
upon rents, vocations, wages of labor, profits,
and commodities. The second and the last
two are all included in the term excise.

After making this classification the author comments as follows:

"As confined to the United States, the scheme
of an income tax arrays itself against the sanctity
of our organic law. It is unqualifiedly unconstitutional. Our table places an income tax under the
head of direct taxation, and there it unqualifiedly
belongs. No authority of any weight has ever
denied the proposition. All direct taxes must be
laid upon the basis of the representative population, as distinguished from the other general canon
therein given of uniformity. The income tax,
however, was laid upon the basis of uniformity,
without regard to the extent of the representative
population, all incomes having been levied upon
wherever found."

The opposite view is taken by Professor Bascom
in his *Growth of Nationality in the United States*,[1]
and vigorously defended. In his criticism of the
Pollock case, he says:

"It is not easy to find another decision which so
openly departs from the law in order to shelter

[1] P. 192.

13

privilege. The technical ground on which this
was done was that a tax on income, derived from
real estate, is a tax on real estate. A logical relation is thus made to push aside a plain, practical
fact, that had long been accepted, and this with
no other result than to embarrass the government
and restrain it in pursuit of justice. An income
tax as a tax,—the only relation in which we have
occasion to consider it—is wholly distinct in form
and substance from a tax on real estate. Its relations as a tax are quite its own, and it carries with
it as significant and beneficent results as any tax
whatever. If we were to divide up an income tax
according to the sources from which an income is
derived, we might dissolve away its own characteristics and assign it a great variety of forms and
qualities. If the income arose from traffic, it
would assume the character of a license; or if the
trade were foreign trade the nature of a duty. If
it were derived from production, its effects would
be those of an excise. Against this subtle reasoning, shaped to sustain an object, there remains the
simple fact that an income tax, a tax of its own
order with its own results, has been repeatedly
recognized, and was able, in a high degree, to
subserve the public welfare."

A similar view was held by Senator Bailey of
Texas. He introduced an amendment to the
Paine Tariff Bill in the form of an income tax
which he believed would be upheld by the courts,
should the amendment have been incorporated
in the bill and passed by Congress. Senator
Bailey, in a notable speech delivered in the
United States Senate on April 26 and 27, 1909,

laid much stress on the soundness of the opinion in the Hylton and Springer cases, and contended that the second opinion in the Pollock case, which went so far as to declare that a tax on personal property was a direct tax and therefore unconstitutional, was, not only in conflict with the Springer case, but that it was in hopeless conflict with the first opinion in the Pollock case.

"Not only is the second decision in the Pollock case in hopeless and irreconcilable conflict with the Springer case but it is inconsistent with the first opinion in the Pollock case. It is true enough that the Court equally divided on the question as to whether a tax on the income of personal property is a direct tax, and the four judges who voted to affirm that doctrine in the first case are not embarrassed by the decision upon the rehearing; but in the opinion, Chief Justice Fuller, speaking for his brothers who agreed with him, excused them for refusing to hold that a tax on the income from personal property was direct after they had decided that an income on real estate was a direct tax. This is his language:

"'We admit that it may not unreasonably be said that logically, if taxes on the rents, issues, and profits of real estate are equivalent to taxes on real estate, and are therefore direct taxes, taxes on the income of personal property as such are equivalent to taxes on such property, and therefore direct taxes. But we are considering the rule *stare decisis* and we must decline to hold ourselves bound to extend the scope of decisions.'

"Thus, Mr. President, the Court, in that first opinion conceded that the uniform decisions have been that a tax on the income of personal property is not a direct tax; but one of the justices had now changed his opinion, and these cases were to be reversed."

But the difficulty of drawing a bill that would clearly meet the objections raised by the Supreme Court became increasingly apparent. The Democrats had attempted to include an income-tax provision in several excise tax bills, and it was becoming more and more a conviction that this was "an attempt to evade the judicial interpretation of the Constitution," and to make a tax measure at the same time both a direct and an indirect tax.[1] This was what the New York *Evening Post* characterized as an unworthy piece of "Legislative quibbling." The Democratic Excise Tax Bill (The Underwood Bill) of 1912 omitted the income tax feature and the House Ways and Means Committee did not report in favor of an income tax section, and gave the following as the reasons:

"First. Because the Supreme Court has declared a general income-tax law unconstitutional for lack of apportionment, and provision has been made whereby the states are now considering the acceptance or rejection of the proposed Sixteenth Amendment to the Constitution giving Congress undisputed authority to impose such a general tax.

[1] See *The Literary Digest*, vol. xliv., No. 13, issue of March 30, 1912.

"Second. Because through the decision of the Supreme Court in upholding the constitutionality of the existing Corporation Tax Law the committee has conceived the idea of extending its provisions as proposed, and to obtain in this way the practical results of an income-tax law without violating the ruling of the Supreme Court in rejecting the Income Tax Law of 1894."

The Sixteenth Amendment was proposed by Congress in 1909, and ratified by the required number of states in February, 1913. The proposed amendment as submitted to the states by Congress reads as follows:

"The Congress shall have power to lay and collect taxes on incomes, from whatever source derived, without apportionment among the several states and without regard to any census or enumeration."

The process of ratification by the required three-fourths (thirty-six) of the state legislatures consumed almost four years from the time of its submission. A favorable vote by thirty-nine state legislatures only shows that the sentiment for the amendment was by no means unanimous. The South and West are responsible for the existence of the amendment. The opposition came largely from the Northeast[1] where only Maine, Maryland, and New York took favorable action of those

[1] The New England view-point is well illustrated by William Lyon Phelps of Yale in an article on "The Income Tax" in the *Independent* for September 19, 1913.

states east of the Alleghany Mountains and north of the Potomac; and New York's favorable vote was due to the Democratic administration that happened to be in power. The amendment was weakest in New England where protectionist influence was strongest. The real difficulty connected with the changing of our organic law is thus realized when we consider the conflicting interests that must be taken into account, and the length of time necessary to secure ratification. This amendment represents the first change in our organic law in forty-three years, and seems to represent the Nation's answer to the Supreme Court's decision of eighteen years ago, that declared an income tax unconstitutional. These periods of time, together with the fact that it required four years to secure ratification of the amendment, supply ample justification for the American doctrine of loose construction.

The Sixteenth Amendment permits, but it does not command, the levy of an income tax. But the Democrats have sought the exercise of this power because they have been committed to the downward revision of our tariff schedules, and they sought to use the proceeds derived from an income tax to make up the loss in governmental revenues as a result of reductions in tariff duties. So, as we naturally expected, the Democrats were not slow to make use of the power granted by the Sixteenth Amendment. Even before the amendment had been officially declared adopted, the Ways and

Means Committee of the House of Representatives had allotted to Representative Cordell Hull, of Tennessee, the author of the Excise-Tax Law, the duty of drafting an income-tax bill, and on October 13, 1913, this bill was placed on the statute books of the United States. The law has been attacked on the ground that it presents many complexities. A recent writer[1] has said: "The ablest lawyers, the most experienced and astute business men, the most careful students and writers fail utterly to agree as to its interpretation and scope." One of the principal contentions of the opponents of the law is that it is discriminatory in that it imposes a special tax on only about 430,000 persons in the country. The author of the law denies this contention, and says that "if this is the chief criticism of the act the country may rest assured that the validity of the statute will be upheld by the Supreme Court." It is safe to predict that the constitutionality of the law will not be long in question, but like other complicated and political statutes, legal attacks will be made on it, and the courts will be required to pass on its application and administration. But with this exception we may safely consider the question of an income tax a settled political issue in this country.

The manner of settlement of the political phases

[1] Mr. Benjamin S. Orcutt on the "Complexities of the Income Tax," in the *American Review of Reviews*, vol. xlix., for January, 1913.

of an income tax represents more perfectly the logical process in the adjustment of political differences than is to be found in the history of any other political question. Starting as a political issue, enacted into law, and tested as to its constitutionality by the Supreme Court, and by this tribunal declared not to be in harmony with the Constitution, it was ultimately, as a result of a platform demand of the Democratic party in 1908, to be submitted to the American people in the form of an amendment, and by them to be made a part of the Constitution itself. Thus, this political issue was, in due course of time, to pass successively through every stage of transition open to a political issue in reaching final confirmation and solution. No other fundamental question in American politics has been carried beyond the solemn conclusions of the Supreme Court, with the exception of the issue of slavery, and in rejecting the peaceful method provided by the Constitution for the ultimate solution of political differences, the American people found themselves compelled to resort to the only other means open to them, i. e., an appeal to arms. Not the least benefit that will result from the final solution of the income-tax question will be the illustration that it has given of the effectiveness of the method provided in our Federal Constitution for satisfactorily adjusting our important differences by legal and peaceful means.

CHAPTER X

THE THEORY OF DIRECT LEGISLATION

THE belief in the theory and possibilities of direct legislation has been growing in popular favor in this country in the last few years. It was first advocated in recent times by the "Grange," and the so-called "People's party" took up the slogan in its first party platform in 1892, and consistently incorporated this doctrine, under the names of the initiative and referendum, in each succeeding platform up to the present time. In the campaign of 1912, the Progressive Republicans made the initiative and referendum a plank in their platform, and President Wilson during the campaign mildly advocated the principle in state and local affairs. The fact that the doctrine has been seriously questioned on the ground that it is subversive of representative government (and on this issue it has been brought to the attention of the Courts) brings the subject within the purview of this discussion.

The idea of direct legislation is an old one, and seems to embody the very essence of democratic self-government. The Ecclesia at Athens, which was established by Solon in the sixth century

B. C., was designed with this idea in mind. It was composed of the citizens who came together to decide such questions as war and peace, and to them were referred such matters as were deemed important by the Council of Four Hundred. The Romans had a similar organ of government during the days of the Republic, known as the *Comitia Tributa*, or assembly of the people by tribes. During the last days of the Republic this became the law-making body. In some of the cantons of Switzerland the *Landesgemeinde*, or gathering of the people is a law-making body, and has been in existence for centuries.[1] To Switzerland we turn to-day for our classic example of direct legislation.[2] An almost exact counterpart of the *Landesgemeinde* of Switzerland is found in the "Town Meeting," which was so common in New England in colonial times. Once each year (or oftener if need be) the voters of the township came together and voted on questions of taxation, expenditure for improvements, and similar matters. The selectmen or township officers were also elected at these meetings. We have no better example of direct

[1] Leacock's *Elements of Political Science*, p. 174 *et seq.* and Woodrow Wilson's *The State*, Section 1361.

[2] The student who is interested in the workings of direct legislation would do well to examine Appendix A of President Lowell's *Public Opinion and Popular Government* (1913). This appendix outlines the subjects on which the referendum and initiative have been taken since the adoption of the general referendum by the constitution of 1874 until 1912, and in the cantons from 1893 to 1910. The vote cast for and against each is also given.

legislation than the type represented by these town meetings.

But the organization of larger and more complex states brought into existence a new type of legislation—that by representation, and for this we are indebted to the Teutons.

"The Teuton," says Woodrow Wilson, "brought into force, particularly in England, the principle of representation, that organization by representative assemblies which enabled the people to act over wide areas through trusted men elected to speak and act in their stead, and which thus enabled the organization of the nation to extend without loss of vitality."[1]

The transition from immediate to representative government is illustrated by Woodrow Wilson[2] with two examples taken from our colonial history. The earliest Legislature of Maryland was composed of all the freemen of the colony; but the next assembly was partly representative, as some of the freemen sent proxies; and for the assemblies thereafter the number of representatives increased and the number of freemen attending in their own right decreased constantly, until it finally became totally representative. The other example is that of Rhode Island which had the early custom of permitting all the citizens to meet in primary assembly at Newport for the purpose of choosing the members of the colonial legislature, after

[1] *The State* (Revised Edition), p. 560.
[2] *Op. cit.*, p. 561.

which they withdrew, leaving the representatives to perform their duties in their representative capacity. While these two illustrations differ in detail, both may be said to represent *missing links* between immediate and representative principles of law-making and government policy.

The principal of constitutional referendum may be said to be a surviving form of the direct system of legislation that has been handed down as a heritage from colonial days. It has been adopted in all the states of the American Union with the single exception of the state of Delaware. The earliest instance of this revival of the principle of direct legislation in its modern form occurred in 1816, when petitions were presented to the General Court[1] of Massachusetts allowing the District of Maine to separate from Massachusetts. In compliance with this request the General Court submitted the question to the qualified voters of the District of Maine with the request that on the twentieth day of May they give in their written votes on the following question to wit: "Shall the Legislature be requested to give its consent to the separation of the District of Maine from Massachusetts proper, and to the erection of said District into a separate State?"[2] This in effect was a constitutional amendment, and is historically important as marking the beginning of the

[1] This was the name of the legislative body (House and Senate). See Constitution of 1780, chapter i., article 1.
[2] Mass. Resolves, Sessions, 1816, p. 148.

revival of the custom of direct legislation by referendum vote.

Statutory referendum became common in many states early in the nineteenth century. In 1821, the General Court of Massachusetts passed "an act establishing the city of Boston," subject, however, to the condition that the act must be approved by the citizens of Boston within twelve days. At this time the General Court passed "an act to regulate the administration of justice within the county of Suffolk,"[1] but this act was declared to be of no effect and void unless the charter was adopted by the people of Boston pursuant to the provisions therein made. Out of this legislation came the first decision designed to test the validity of such legislation. The question came before the Supreme Judicial Court in 1826, and Judge Parker used the following language in passing upon the constitutionality of this statute:

"This objection, for aught we see, stands unsupported by any authority or sound argument. Why may not the Legislature make the existence of any act depend upon the happening of any future event? Constitutions themselves are so made. . . . We see no impropriety, certainly no unconstitutionality, in giving the people the opportunity to accept or reject such provisions."[2]

To Massachusetts belongs the distinction of giving to the world the first example of a popularly

[1] General Laws of Mass., sec. 17.
[2] Wales v. Belcher, 3 Pick., 508.

ratified constitution, and to this state also "belongs the further distinction of having revived and perpetuated the popular legislation of her colonial era."[1]

But statutory referendum became quite widely diffused rather early in the nineteenth century. The public school had been a common subject of discussion at the town meetings of an earlier era, and it was but natural that the legislatures of a later day should be disposed to empower local communities with authority to create schools and provide for their maintenance. In Maryland a statute[2] was passed in 1826 providing for the establishment of a system of primary public instruction, provided a majority of the voters in any county of the state should vote in favor of such primary school instruction. Pennsylvania soon adopted a similar measure.[3] The Constitution[4] of the Texas Republic, adopted in 1836, provided that "no county shall be established unless it be done on the petition of one hundred free male inhabitants."

These examples suffice to show that the principle of direct legislation is not new in America. But in the past the referendum was much more common than the initiative, and the two were never thought of as reciprocal legislative agencies. Public interest in the subject was revived by the

---

[1] See Lobingier's *The People's Law*, p. 197 *et seq.* and p. 349.
[2] Maryland Laws, 1825, chapter 162.
[3] Act of April 15, 1835.　　　　[4] Article IV., section 11.

publication in America of Bryce's *American Commonwealth* in 1888, which made a careful comparative study of American institutions with those of European countries, and the luminous comparison with Switzerland, which is also a republic, made a profound impression on the American people. A more recent study of the subject by Dr. Borgeaud[1] has had a marked effect on the American public mind. It has required only a few years for these academic discussions to pass into practical legislation, and the legislation, in connection with the Court decisions relating to them, will now be briefly reviewed.

The People's party platform of 1892, which was the first national platform of this party, passed a resolution commending "to the thoughtful consideration of the people and the reform press, the legislative system known as the initiative and referendum." This marked the inauguration of this political doctrine in this country. The People's party has continued to incorporate it in each platform since that time, and in the decline of this party's influence, we find the doctrine taken up with renewed zeal by the Progressive Republicans in 1912. It is safe to predict that we will hear much of this subject in political discussion during the next few years.

In the mean time the principle has been gradually working its way into the constitutions of the states of the Union and gaining strength in the

[1] *Rise of Modern Democracy in Old and New England* (1894).

public mind. The first formal adoption in America
of the initiative and referendum in their application to general legislation was the result of a joint
resolution[1] passed by the Legislature of South
Dakota in 1897, which was duly ratified by the
people.[2] Section 2 of this resolution reads as
follows:

"The legislative power of the state shall be
vested in a legislature, which shall consist of a
senate and house of representatives, except that
the people expressly reserve to themselves the right
to propose measures, which measures the legislature shall enact and submit to a vote of the
electors of the state and also the right to require
that any laws which the legislature may have
enacted shall be submitted to a vote of the electors
of the state before going into effect except such
laws as may be necessary for the immediate
preservation of the public peace, health, or safety,
support of the state government and its existing
public institutions."

The section further provides that five per cent.
of the electors by petition may invoke the provisions of the constitution.

Utah was the second state to adopt the principle
of direct legislation. The legislature of this state
submitted to the people a joint resolution[3] proposing an amendment of this kind in 1899. The

[1] South Dakota Laws, 5th Sess., chapter 39.
[2] In November, 1898.
[3] Utah Senate Journal 3d Session, p. 453.

phraseology of this resolution differed somewhat from that of the resolution adopted in South Dakota. It provided that:

"The legal voters, or such fractional part thereof, of the state of Utah as may be provided by law, under such conditions and in such manner and within such time as may be provided by law, may initiate any desired legislation and cause the same to be submitted to a vote of the people for approval or rejection, or may require any law passed by the legislature (except those laws passed by a two-thirds vote of the members elected to each house of the legislature) to be submitted to the voters of the state before such law shall take effect."

This proposal was approved by the people of the state at the election in November, 1900, and by a majority of almost three to one.

Oregon, Nevada, Missouri, Montana, Delaware, Maine, Oklahoma, North Dakota, and Ohio, in the order named, have adopted the initiative and referendum in some form. Oregon began even earlier than Utah to apply this principle, but the constitutional provision requiring action by two successive legislatures retarded somewhat the actual operation of such a plan. This state first proposed a joint resolution in 1899, and it was duly approved by the governor on February 6th of that year. But as it had to come before the Legislature again in 1901, it was not formally submitted to the people for ratification until June, 1902, at which time the amendment was ratified

14

by a majority of about eleven to one. This amendment, together with a similar one, adopted in 1903, has carried the principle of direct legislation further than it has been carried in any other state.[1]

In Missouri the proposed amendment incorporating the initiative and referendum in the constitution was first proposed by the Legislature of that state in 1903. When the matter was submitted to the people, it failed of adoption. This seems to have been the first time such a resolution was defeated when fairly presented to the people for ratification. But the matter was resubmitted by the Legislature in 1907, the phraseology being somewhat different from the earlier resolution, and this time the resolution was adopted by a majority of thirty thousand.

The new State of Oklahoma has the distinction of being the first state to incorporate the initiative and referendum in an original constitution. The article[2] had the effect of retarding the acceptance of the state into the Union by Congress, but the constitution was adopted by the people by an unusual majority.

The adoption of the initiative and referendum in the new constitution of Ohio in 1912, was significant because Ohio has been regarded as one of the more conservative states. This new constitution goes further in some particulars than that of any other state in the application of the principle; especially is this true of the number of

[1] Oregon Laws, 1903, p. 244, sec. 8.   [2] Article V.

petitioners required to invoke a referendum vote, the percentage being only three per cent. of the voters of the state. A writer in a leading magazine has said: "The initiative and referendum amendment, now a part of the Ohio constitution, is more radical and misrepresentative in its operation than the similar measures in any other states of the Union."[1]

This brief description is sufficient to show the nature and extent of the growth of the doctrine of direct legislation in this country. It is easy to see that it has been revived and reëstablished upon the models given us by Switzerland. But in this country the provisions of the constitution of Oregon have been followed very closely. In many cases the phraseology of the Oregon constitution relating to this subject has been appropriated. In brief the essential provisions of the constitution of Oregon are as follows: (1) Legal voters at least equal to eight per cent. may initiate legislation; (2) five per cent. of the voters may cause a referendum to be taken on laws which have been enacted by the legislature; (3) the referendum must be invoked within ninety days; (4) the legislature may on its own motion make operative any law which it may pass only after ratification by the people; (5) exception is made for laws "necessary for the immediate preservation of the public peace, health, or safety"; (6) the veto power of

[1] Ryan's "The Influence of Socialism on the Ohio Constitution," in *The North American Review* for November, 1912, p. 665.

the governor is withheld in all cases of popular ratification or approval. It is seen that the system is merely an alternative one. Law-making by the regularly constituted legislature is not abolished, but merely supplemented with law-making by popular vote, and the latter method is made inoperative in all cases where speedy action is necessary to protect the public interest.[1]

Passing over many unessential details connected with the system, the fate of direct legislation before the courts will be briefly reviewed. The constitutional question involved is that of its effect on representative government. *Does direct legislation abolish or destroy representative government?* Our Federal Constitution provides that "The United States shall guarantee to every state in this Union a Republican form of Government," and the question involved is that of deciding if this implies a representative system to the exclusion of an immediate one. A definition or two will be helpful in the approach to the judicial opinion on the subject:

"Immediate government," says Professor Burgess, "is that form in which the state exercises directly the functions of Government."[2]

"Representative government," says this author "is, in general definition, that form in which the state vests the power of government in an organi-

[1] The works of Oberholtzer, *The Referendum, Initiative, and Recall in America,* and Lobinger's *The People's Law* have been freely consulted in this discussion.

[2] *Political Science and Constitutional Law,* vol. ii., p. 1.

zation or in organizations more or less distinct from its own organization."[1]

Professor Garner says: "Where the sovereign has delegated to an organ or organs the power to act for it in matters of government, as is now the almost universal practice, we have representative government in some form."[2]

"We mean by representative government," says Lord Brougham,[3] "one in which the body of the people, either in whole or in a considerable proportion of the whole, elect their deputies to a chamber of their own." These definitions are sufficient to indicate the academic teaching on the subject. The view of the courts will now be studied in the light of these definitions.

The constitutionality of direct legislation was promptly and completely affirmed in the state courts of Oregon at the first opportunity. The first case involving this principle reached the Supreme Court of Oregon in 1903. This was in the case of Kadderly v. Portland[4] and the amendment was assailed on the grounds that it violated that provision of the Federal Constitution that guaranteed to each state "a republican form of government." The court in an exhaustive opinion upheld the amendment in every particular, answering the constitutional objection in this emphatic language:

[1] *Op. cit.*, vol. ii., p. 2.
[2] *Introduction to Political Science*, p. 179.
[3] "British Constitution," *Works*, vol. ii., p. 89.
[4] 44 Oregon, 118.

"The initiative and referendum amendment does not abolish or destroy the republican form of government or substitute another in its place. The representative character of the government still remains. The people have simply reserved to themselves a larger share of legislative power."

This opinion has been twice reaffirmed by the Supreme Court of Oregon, first, in 1909, in the case of Oregon v. Pacific States Telephone and Telegraph Company,[1] and second, in the case of Kiernan v. City of Portland,[2] the decision being rendered in this case in 1910. The Court in the latter case took an excursion into history and quoted from some of the founders of our Government. For instance, we are reminded that James Wilson defined a republic as a government constructed on the belief "that the supreme power resides in the body of the people," and Jefferson is quoted as defining a republic as a government "by its citizens in mass acting directly and not personally according to rules established by the majority," and the Court concludes that Oregon has not departed from the path marked out by the fathers of our Republic in adopting the principle of the initiative and the referendum.

An important precedent has been established in the state of Oklahoma in the case of *ex-parte* Wagner,[3] where the principle of direct legislation is upheld on the grounds that it was a part of the constitution when the state came into the Union.

[1] 53 Oregon, 162.   [2] 112 Pacific, 402.   [3] 21 Oklahoma, 33.

The Court recites the fact that the Constitution requires that each state entering the Union shall "be republican in form," that the constitution adopted and submitted to Congress contained a provision relating to the initiative and the referendum, and that on November 16, 1907, President Roosevelt proclaimed Oklahoma a state of the Union, declaring at the same time the "said Constitution and government of the proposed state of Oklahoma to be republican in form."

The Supreme Court of California makes an important point in the case of In re Pfahler,[1] which arose out of the Home Rule charter of Los Angeles, the decision regarding which was rendered in 1906. The Court calls attention to the provision of the Federal Constitution guaranteeing to each state a republican form of government, and then reminds us that it was a fact well-known to the members of the Federal Convention that the town-meeting legislative system prevailed in some of the states at that time, and that there was no intention to bring into question the validity of the system by the adoption of the Constitution. The Court made it plain that it did not wish "to be understood as intimating that the people of a state may not reserve the supervisory control as to general state legislation afforded by the initiative and referendum without violating this provision (art. LV., sec. 4) of the Constitution."

[1] 150 California, 71.

In Hopkins *v*. City of Duluth,[1] a Minnesota case decided in 1900, this language is used:

"We apprehend that a little reflection must satisfy any one that the advantage of providing local self-government by the voters directly interested through a referendum is abstractly, as well as concretely, more republican than through representatives of the people in the Legislature, many of whom are not at all interested in the affairs of the local community. . . . The test of republican or democratic government is the will of the people expressed in majorities under the proper forms of law. . . . So long as the ultimatum of decision is left to the will of the people at the ballot-box, it (the Government) is essentially republican."

No deliverance, as yet, has been made by the Supreme Court on this subject, but we have important opinions from that Court on the general question of the nature of a republican form of government that may indicate very definitely what we may expect when this question comes up for review by our highest Federal Court. In 1874, Chief Justice Waite delivered the opinion in the case of Minor *v*. Happersett,[2] in which this language was used:

"The guarantee is of a republican form of government. No particular government is designated as republican; neither is the exact form to be guaranteed in any manner especially designated. Here, as in other parts of the instrument [the

[1] 81 Minnesota, 189. [2] 21 Wall, 162.

Constitution], we are compelled to resort elsewhere to ascertain what was intended.
"The guarantee necessarily implies a duty on
the part of the states themselves to provide such
a government. All the states had governments
when the Constitution was adopted. In all the
people participated to some extent through their
representatives elected in the manner specially
provided. These governments the Constitution
did not change. They were accepted precisely as
they were, and it is therefore to be presumed that
they were such as it was the duty of the states to
provide. Thus we have unmistakable evidence
of what was republican in form within the meaning of that term as employed in the Constitution."

Cooley[1] lays down the same principle in the
following words:

"The Constitution of the United States assumes
the existence of thirteen distinct state governments, over whose people its authority was to be
extended if ratified by conventions chosen for the
purpose. Each of these states was then exercising
the powers of government under some form of
written constitution, and that instrument would
remain unaffected by the adoption of the national
Constitution, except in those particulars in which
the two would come in conflict; and as to those,
the latter would modify and control the former."

But as a matter of fact, we have no instance
where a state, after the adoption of the national
Constitution, found it necessary to modify its con-

[1] *Constitutional Limitations* (Sixth Edition), chapter iii., p. 42.

stitution in order to bring the state organic law into harmony with the organic law of the Nation.

A rather important paragraph relating to the nature of representative government occurs in the decision of In re Duncan,[1] which was rendered by Chief Justice Fuller in 1891. This is the language used:

"By the Constitution a republican form of government is guaranteed to every state in the Union, and the distinguishing feature of the form is the right of the people to choose their own officers for governmental administration and pass their own laws in virtue of the legislative power reposed in representative bodies whose legitimate acts may be said to be those of the people themselves."

It is necessary at this point to remind the reader of a distinction between the principle of direct legislation in local districts or municipalities and that which comprehends and affects the entire jurisdiction of the state. It is a settled principle of constitutional law that the power conferred on the Legislature to make laws cannot be delegated to other agencies,[2] unless the sovereign power that conferred this authority upon the Legislature should by some formal act decide to provide for such a

[1] 139 U. S., p. 449.
[2] See Cooley's *Constitutional Limitations* (Sixth Edition), p. 137. Also Locke (*On Civil Government*): "The Legislature neither must nor can transfer the power of making laws to anybody else, or place it anywhere but where the people have." (Section 142.) Cooley also gives an important list of decisions in which this doctrine is maintained.

delegation of power. But the courts have been disposed to hold that municipal organizations are mere auxiliaries of the state governments, and that the re-delegation of the law-making power to such organizations is not in reality a delegation of the power conferred upon the Legislature by the sovereign will of the people of the state.

The ability of the courts to uphold the delegation of legislative functions to local governmental organs has resulted from the principle of our laws that gives validity to conditional enactments; *i. e.*, those that have been passed by a legislative body but whose effect depends upon the happening of some future event. This future event may be (1) the "ascertainment of a fact upon which the law makes or intends to make its own action depend," (2) "or on the happening of a certain contingency."[1] This contingency may be the approval of the law by a majority of the qualified voters. The application of this principle has enabled the courts in many states to uphold the principle of law-making by popular vote.

While direct legislation has been upheld where exercised, in local districts, there have been some courts that have denied that such a power can be delegated. Oberholtzer,[2] the leading authority on this subject, says that previous to 1850, eight

---

[1] 26 Wisconsin, 291. This principle is discussed also by Cooley (*op. cit.*), p. 137 *et seq.* This author also gives a long list of citations in which the doctrine is upheld beginning with the case of Brig *Aurora v.* U. S., 7 Cranch, p. 382.

[2] *Op. cit.*, chapter xiii.

opinions had been delivered in which the validity of the local referendum was involved.

"Of these eight, three relate to the prohibition of the liquor traffic, three to taxation or the public subscription of stock to private companies, and two to other questions of local government. In six of the eight cases the validity of this method of submitting local laws to popular vote was affirmed, and in two, both cases arising out of local option laws, it was denied."

This author says that since 1850 this type of legislation has been denied validity in only four states. These are Iowa, Indiana, California, and Texas, the first-named state having consistently denied the principle in a long line of decisions. In concluding his chapter on the constitutionality of the local referendum, Oberholtzer makes use of the following language:

"The judges pass almost imperceptibly from one to the other [from the contingency theory to the theory that the municipality is a mere auxiliary to the state Legislature and that legislation by it is not a re-delegation of law-making power] and whatever their own individual views may be as to the law in the case, they are at any rate compelled to recognize that conditional legislation of this kind has existed in all parts of the Republic from the foundation of the government. Whether there is in a strict judicial sense justification for it or not, it is here and it must be reckoned with as a part of us. A great weight of precedent and, perhaps other important considerations, which are not empirical, can be appealed to in its defence. The town meeting and the referendum are factors in the American system of local government which will remain with us long after the jurist has ceased to seek the grounds for these interesting political institutions."

But an entirely different principle applies with reference to the referendum on general state laws. In the previous cases cited which sustain such laws, we find that the constitutions specially authorized such legislation. It seems to be a well-established principle of American law that unless there is expressed constitutional authority for the Legislature to delegate the law-making power to the people of the state, no such power can exist. This question was submitted to the Supreme Court of Massachusetts by the Legislature of that state, and the majority of the Court was of the opinion that a general statute submitted to the voters of the state was unauthorized by law and, therefore, unconstitutional. But the Court in answer to another question propounded by the Legislature at the same time relating to law-making by local districts answered in the affirmative, expressing the opinion that in general such enactments would be constitutional. This doubtless will eventually become the generally recognized doctrine in all the states of the Union.

One other question suggests itself with reference to direct legislation: Does it in practice operate to secure representative government? Of course, this question will be answered in opposite ways by the advocates and opponents of this method of legislation, but a brief reference to these opinions may be in order.

A leading paper of Portland, Oregon,[1] which was at first an advocate of the initiative and referendum, condemned it in practice in the following language:

"It was not intended that representative government should be abolished by the new system; but it has been abolished by it. Any group of persons, from the cave of Adullam, or other groups of persons of ill-arranged intellects, can propose initiative measures or call the referendum; and there is danger always that the crudest measures may pass into law through the inattention of the voters, or that proper legislative measures may be turned down through the referendum. . . . Representative government is after all, a pretty good thing. Oregon will yet return to it."

Professor Stimson, a leading authority on comparative legislation, and an instructor in this field in Harvard University, condemns the principle of direct legislation in the following words:

"Direct legislation," says this authority, "has been very popular as a political slogan during the past few years, but it has not been adopted as yet in any of the thirteen original states. The objections to it are fundamentally that it destroys the principle of representative government; that it takes responsibility from the Legislature with

[1] *The Oregonian.*

the result, probably, of getting a more and more inferior type of man as state representative; that it is unnecessary, inasmuch as any one may have any bill introduced in the Legislature to-day, and public sentiment be effectual to prevent the bill from being defeated; and finally, the objection of inconvenience, that it is cumbrous and unmanageable to work."[1]

In opposition to these opinions we have that of United States Senator Jonathan Bourne,[2] himself a Senator from Oregon. In discussing popular government in Oregon, he says that his state "has evolved the best known system of popular government" in this country.

"The initiative," says he, "develops the electorate, placing directly upon them the responsibility for legislation enacted under its provision; the referendum elevates the Legislature because of the possibility of its use in case of undesirable legislation. Brains, ideas, and argument, rather than money, intimidation, and log-rolling, govern the standards of legislation. . . . Results obtained under direct legislation, in Oregon, compare so favorably with the work of a legislative assembly that an effort to repeal the initiative and referendum would be overwhelmingly defeated. No effort has ever been attempted."

Mr. Roosevelt says[3] that "unquestionably an

[1] *Popular Law-making*, p. 295.

[2] See his article on "Popular Government in Oregon," in the *Outlook*, vol. xcvi., p. 321, also Speech U. S. Senate on May 5, 1910.

[3] "Nationalism and Popular Rule" in the *Outlook*, vol. xcvii., p. 96.

ideal representative body is the best imaginable legislative body," but "I believe," says he, "that it would be a good thing to have the principle of the initiative and the referendum applied in most of our states. . . . In other words, if the Legislature fails to act one way or the other on some bill as to which there is a genuine popular demand, then there should unquestionably be power in the people through the initiative to compel such action. Similarly, on any bill important enough to arouse genuine public interest there should be power for the people to insist upon the bill being referred to popular vote, so that the constituents may authoritatively determine whether or not their representatives have misrepresented them."

Mr. Roosevelt also calls attention to this important limitation of the practice of direct legislation in the same article: "This, of course, does not necessarily mean that the principle would work equally well in all other communities, and under our system it is difficult to see at present how it could normally have more than state-wide application."

The advantages and disadvantages of the system have been ably summarized by Professor Gettell[1] as follows:

"Among the advantages of direct legislation may be noted:
"1. The people may force action upon apathetic legislatures, or may prevent legislation that does not reflect the wishes of the community.

[1] *Introduction to Political Science*, p. 215.

"2. The people are less likely than the Legislature to be improperly influenced or to hesitate in opposing certain special interests.

"3. Public sentiment is awakened and interest in government stimulated if voters have questions of importance to consider.

"4. The local referendum may adapt general laws to the needs of particular localities.

"Among the disadvantages are:

"1. Voters take little interest in such elections . . .

"2. The referendum destroys the sense of responsibilities of legislatures and executives . . .

"3. It is almost impossible to frame complicated statutes concerning economic or social questions in such a way that a simple yes or no will indicate the real will of the people.'"

The voters of the various states have practically become a fourth department of government, in which the functions of the other three are more and more coming to be exercised. The oldest function of the electorate was executive, in which it exercised the power to elect its representatives; through the initiative and the referendum it is now exercising in larger measure the function of legislation; and in the proposed theory of the recall of judicial decisions, the electorate will become in some important respects at least the court of last resort in the interpretation of our laws. The following and concluding chapter will briefly discuss this novel and remarkable theory.

15

CHAPTER XI

THE THEORY OF THE RECALL OF JUDICIAL DECISIONS

THE theory of the recall of decisions may be said to be the natural result of more than a century's teaching by the courts of this country that they possessed the power to declare the laws passed by the state and national legislatures unconstitutional when such enactments were deemed to be in conflict with the organic law of either the state or the Nation. As has been previously shown this doctrine has been questioned by statesmen from the earliest days of the Republic. Jefferson had this assumption of power by the courts in mind when he used the following language: "The judiciary of the United States is the subtle corps of sappers and miners constantly working underground to undermine the foundations of our confederated fabric," and Professor Burgess in discussing this doctrine in a recent work speaks of the Supreme Court as the "aristocracy of the robe."[1] It has been a popular belief throughout our history as a nation that the power of the judiciary to annul a statute on the grounds of unconstitutionality made the judiciary not a co-

[1] *Political Science and Constitutional Law*, vol. ii., p. 365.

ordinate branch of government, but placed the other two in a position of subordination in some respects at least. To escape from this supremacy of the judiciary, and to restore the coördination in practice as the fathers had decreed in theory has been under consideration at various times since Marshall first laid down the doctrine in the historic decision of Marbury *v.* Madison in 1803.

The friends of the recent theory of the recall of judicial decisions claim to have found a precedent for such a theory in the history of the Eleventh Amendment to our Federal Constitution. Before this amendment was passed, a suit was brought by an individual against the State of Georgia, and the Supreme Court promptly held that such a suit could be maintained in the courts of the United States. The decision aroused opposition on the part of the people, and, as a result, the Eleventh Amendment, denying this power, was duly submitted by Congress and in due time (1788) adopted by the people.

"This amendment," it is stated in an editorial in the *Outlook*, "did not in terms alter the Constitution. It simply declared that the Constitution should not be construed as the Supreme Court of the United States had construed it. And in subsequent proceedings the Supreme Court unanimously recognized the right of the people to adopt this amendment, and so, in effect, though not in form, to reverse their previous decision. In fact, it did in form as well as in effect reverse their interpretation of the Constitution."[1]

This view is practically borne out by Justice Bradley in a reference to this early case in an opinion delivered by him in the case of Hans *v.* Louisiana. In discussing the right of a citizen to sue a state, he said:

"That decision was made in the case of Chisholm *v.* Georgia (2 Dallas, 419); and created such a shock of surprise throughout the country that, at the first meeting of Congress thereafter, the Eleventh Amendment to the Constitution was almost unanimously proposed, and was in due course adopted by the legislatures of the states. This amendment, expressing the will of the ultimate sovereignty of the whole country, superior to all legislatures and all courts, actually reversed the decision of the Supreme Court. It did not in terms prohibit suits by individuals against the states, but declared that the Constitution should not be construed to import any power to authorize the bringing of such suits. The language of the amendment is that 'the judicial power of the United States shall not be construed to extend to any suit in law or equity commenced or prosecuted against one of the United States by citizens of another state, or by citizens or subjects of any foreign state.' The Supreme Court had construed the judicial power as extending to such a suit, and its decision was thus overruled. The Court itself so understood the effect of the amendment for after its adoption Attorney-General Lee, in the case of Hollingsworth *v.* Virginia (3 Dallas, 378),

[1] *Outlook*, vol. ci., p. 59.

submitted this question to the Court: 'Whether
the amendment did or did not supersede all suits
pending, as well as prevent the institution of new
suits, against any one of the United States by
citizens of another State?' Tilghman and Rawle
argued in the negative, contending that the jurisdiction of the Court was unimpaired in relation to
all suits instituted previous to the adoption of
the amendment. But on the succeeding day the
Court delivered a unanimous opinion that 'the
amendment being constitutionally adopted, there
could not be exercised any jurisdiction in any case,
past or future, in which a State was sued by the
citizens of another State, or by citizens or subjects
of any foreign state.' "[1]

Mr. Roosevelt stated in his now famous speech
before the Ohio Constitutional Convention that
Lincoln advocated this doctrine with reference
to the Dred Scott decision, but a close study of
the words of Lincoln does not seem to fully justify
this conclusion. The words of Lincoln referred to
by Mr. Roosevelt occurred in a speech delivered
at Springfield, Illinois, on June 26, 1857, when
this language was used:

"We believe as much as Judge Douglas—
perhaps more—in obedience to and respect for
the judicial department of government.

"We think its decisions on Constitutional questions, when fully settled, should control, not only
the particular cases decided, but the general
policy of the country, subject to be disturbed only
by amendments to the Constitution as provided

[1] See *Outlook*, vol. ci., p. 59.

in that instrument itself. More than this would be revolution.

"But we think the Dred Scott decision to be erroneous. We know the Court that has made it has overruled its own decisions, and we shall do what we can to have it overrule this."

It is difficult to read into these words the theory of the recall of judicial decisions as advocated by Mr. Roosevelt, for it is quite clear that Mr. Lincoln hoped only to induce the Court acting within its own constitutional prerogative to reverse in later decisions its own opinion in the case referred to.[1] Lincoln could not have had in mind reversal of judicial opinion by popular election.[2]

The recall of judges is the last step in the theory of the recall of public officials which was first formally advocated by the "People's Party." This party had from its origin advocated direct legislation through the initiative and the referendum, but in its platform of 1900 it went a step further and added this phrase to the plank concerning the initiative and referendum "and to recall unfaithful public servants." This theory gained great prominence and emphasis in each platform and campaign of this party from that year on. The theory of the recall of judges did

---

[1] The views of Lincoln on this subject are ably presented in a chapter on "Lincoln and Judicial Supremacy" in Haines' "The American Doctrine of Judicial Supremacy" (1913), p. 204 et seq.

[2] See views of Mr. H. W. Stillman expressed in Outlook, vol. cii., p. 251.

not become a vital issue until Arizona and New Mexico sought admission to statehood into the Union. The resolution that was submitted to Congress contained an amendment to the Arizona constitution, providing for the recall of the judiciary by popular vote, and this provision caused a bitter fight to be made on the resolution. More than a score of the leading members of Congress took part in the debate. Both Democratic and Republican members joined in condemning the provision of the Arizona constitution that related to the recall of the judiciary. Mr. Samuel W. McCall, Republican from Massachusetts, declared that the popular recall of judges "would not only in the long run result in the destruction of a republican form of government, but would be entirely subversive of civil government." Mr. Littleton, Democrat from New York, was equally vehement in opposition to the measure. But the resolution admitting Arizona and New Mexico to statehood was finally adopted on May 23, 1911, by the decisive majority of 214 to 57. Many of those who were opposed to the recall provision finally voted for the resolution.

Many of the most thoughtful men of the Nation have doubted the wisdom of the recall of judges by popular vote. Still the principle has gained rather wide application. At the present time Oregon, California, Arizona, Arkansas, Idaho, and Nevada have a state wide recall, which includes in its scope every public official. North Dakota and Wisconsin have passed recall amendments which will be voted on at an early date. No practical attempt has been made as yet to recall a judge, but that we will have such a recall before a great while is almost certain.

Regardless of the growing popularity of the principle of the recall, and especially the recall of judges, the obvious dangers and imperfections of such a practice has caused a few political leaders to seek a remedy that will accomplish the same ends without at the same time encountering the dangers and imperfections incidental to the recall system. Mr. Roosevelt startled the country early in 1912, in a speech of unusual interest, by proposing a substitute for the recall of judges by popular vote. He suggested that instead of recalling the judge, whose error was probably of the head instead of the heart, that the people by popular vote recall the decision that had proved offensive and subversive of the ends of social justice. The theory is so novel and interesting as to justify a rather extended quotation from the speech of Mr. Roosevelt.

In his preliminary discussion, Mr. Roosevelt defines his position with reference to the recall of judges:

"I do not believe in adopting the recall [of judges] save as a last resort, when it has become clearly evident that no other course will achieve the desired result. But either the recall will have to be adopted or else it will have to be made much easier than it now is to get rid, not merely of a bad judge, but a judge who, however virtuous, has grown so out of touch with social needs and facts that he is unfit longer to render good service on the bench. It is nonsense to say that impeachment meets the difficulty. . . . Impeachment as a remedy for the ills of which the people justly complain is a complete failure. A quicker, a more summary, remedy is needed. . . . And whenever it be found in actual practice that such remedy does not give the needed results, I would unhesitatingly adopt the recall.

"But there is one kind of recall in which I very earnestly believe, and the immediate adoption of which I urge. . . . When a judge decides a constitutional question, when he decides what the people as a whole can or cannot do, the people should have the right to recall that decision if they think it wrong. . . . What the Supreme Court of the Nation decides to be law binds both the national and the state courts, and all the people within the boundaries of the Nation. But the decision of a state court on a constitutional question should be subject to revision by the people of the state. Again and again in the past justice has been scandalously obstructed by state courts declaring state laws in conflict with the Federal Constitution, although the Supreme Court of the Nation had never so decided or had even decided in a contrary sense. When the Supreme Court of the state declares a given statute unconstitutional, because in conflict with the state or the national Constitution, its opinion should be subject to revision by the people themselves. Such an opinion ought always to be treated with great respect by the people, and unquestionably in the majority of cases would be accepted and followed by them. But actual experience has shown the vital need of the people reserving to themselves the right to pass upon such opinion. If any considerable number of the people feel that the decision is in defiance of justice, they should be given the right by petition to bring before the voters at some subsequent election, special or otherwise, as might be decided, and after the fullest opportunity for deliberation and debate, the question whether or not the judges' interpretation of the Constitution is to be sustained. If it is sustained, well and good. If not, then the popular verdict is to be accepted as final, the decision is to be treated as reversed and the construction of the Constitution definitely decided subject only to action by the Supreme Court of the United States."

The announcement and formulation of the doctrine of the recall of judicial decisions as in the Columbus speech of Mr. Roosevelt aroused widespread interest in his theory. Newspapers and public men throughout the country discussed the question from every possible view-point. Many prominent men of both the leading parties condemned this novel scheme, and leading newspapers both partisan and independent, declared it to be visionary and impractical. These criticisms caused Mr. Roosevelt to reply in a notable address delivered at Carnegie Hall, New York City, under the auspices of the Civic Forum, on the evening of March 20, 1912. He took for his subject, "The Right of the People to Rule," and devoted much of his address to the question of the recall of judicial decisions, answering especially the criticisms of President Taft. In order to make his position as clear as possible Mr. Roosevelt in this speech summarizes his position in the following words:

(1) "I am not proposing anything in connection with the Supreme Court of the United States, or with the Federal Constitution.

(2) "I am not proposing anything having any connection with ordinary suits, civil or criminal, as between individuals.

(3) "I am not speaking of the recall of judges.

(4) "I am proposing merely that in a certain class of cases involving the police power, when a state court has set aside as unconstitutional a law passed by the Legislature for the general welfare, the question of the validity of the law,—which should depend as Justice Holmes so well phrases it, upon the prevailing morality of preponderant opinion—be submitted for final determination to a vote of the people, taken after due time for consideration. And I contend that the people, in the nature of things, must be better judges of what is the preponderant opinion than the courts, and that the courts should not be allowed to reverse the political philosophy of the people."

Mr. Roosevelt in both of these speeches—the Columbus speech and the Carnegie Hall speech—supported his unique theory with some rather remarkable argument. In the former speech he used this striking line of thought.

"Remember, when I am asking the people themselves in the last resort to interpret the law which they themselves have made, that after all I am only asking that they step in and authoritatively reconcile the conflicting decisions of the courts. In all these cases the judges and the courts have decided every which way, and it is foolish to talk of the sanctity of a judge-made law which half the judges strongly denounce. If there must be decision by a close majority, then let the people step in and let it be their decision that decides."

The opposition that developed to this doctrine brought out some interesting comments. Mr. Taft condemned the doctrine in no uncertain terms. He declared that such a theory "is utterly without merit or utility, and, instead of being . . . in the interest of all the people, and of the stability of popular government, is sowing the seed of confusion and tyranny," and again in a striking passage he says this teaching "lays the ax at the foot of the tree of well-ordered freedom, and subjects the guarantees of life, liberty, and property without remedy to the fitful impulse of a temporary majority of an electorate." The majority of the leading members of the Republican party agreed with the opposition to the proposal of Mr. Roosevelt, among these being such men as Senator Root, Senator Lodge, and Ex-Secretary Nagle.

But after the split in the Republican party at the Chicago Convention in 1913, and the formation of the so-called Progressive Republican party, the line was clearly drawn on the issue of the theory of the recall of judicial decisions; and as

we naturally would have expected, this theory
became a plank in the Progressive platform when
the Progressives met at Chicago in the late
summer of 1912. The declaration on this subject
reads as follows:

"The Progressive party demands such restrictions of the power of the courts as shall leave to
the people the ultimate authority to determine
fundamental questions of social welfare and public
policy. To secure this end it pledges itself to
provide:

(1) "That when an act passed under the police
power of the state is held unconstitutional under
the state constitution by the courts, the people,
after an ample interval for deliberation, shall have
an opportunity to vote on the question whether
they desire the act to become law notwithstanding
such decision.

(2) "That every decision of the highest appellate court of a state declaring an act of the
Legislature unconstitutional on the ground of its
violation of fundamental law shall be subject to
the same review by the Supreme Court of the
United States as is now accorded to decisions
sustaining such legislation."

The popular review of judicial decisions on laws
for securing social justice became an important
issue in their campaign before the people, but the
regular Republicans and the Democrats did not
take the issue seriously, and both devoted most of
their attention to questions deemed by them of
more immediate concern to the people.

The student of political science must be interested in the real merits of such a proposal as that presented by the recall of judicial decisions. There have been very few judicial discussions presented on the merits of this theory. Most of the arguments offered and the views expressed are obviously partisan and emanate from men of pronounced political views or from newspapers that are definitely aligned with one or the other of the leading political parties. An exception to this is found in an article in the *Atlantic*[1] on "The Significance of the Recall of Judicial Decisions," by Mr. Karl T. Frederick of the New York Bar. The author in his introduction says, "The purpose of the writer is neither to defend the recall of Judicial Decisions, nor to abuse it, but rather to examine it, and to get at its more important qualities and characteristics."

In this article this proposal is compared with that of the recall of judges, and the question is asked: "Is it a genuine correction of the evil it is aiming to prevent?" He declares that it is superior to the recall of judges.

"The Recall of Decisions is in these respects undoubtedly more precise and effective. The question is more clear cut and easily understood. Shall a decision nullify a particular legislative act upon constitutional grounds and remain the law, or shall it be in substance overruled? The ques-

[1] Vol cx., p. 46 (issue for July, 1912).

tion is shifted from men to principles, and the issue is made impersonal and concrete."

An examination of the question on its merits leads this writer to the conclusion that after all, "Whether the Recall of Decisions should be adopted, is, like most other political questions, purely one of expediency."

But it seems that the theory of the recall of judicial decisions is a matter of more serious concern and of greater importance than Mr. Frederick would have us believe. Viewed in the light of its historical relations, it is the first rational expedient, if it be an expedient at all, that has been offered as a substitute for the well-established doctrine that the courts have the power to declare statutes unconstitutional, and in opposition to which there is a growing sentiment in the ranks of American citizens of all political faiths. The conclusion reached by Mr. Harold Remington[1] in a short, but forceful, argument in favor of the theory may be more nearly the one that comprehends the significance of the question: "Perhaps," says he, "are thus to be solved many of those grave questions looming up to menace our future which the deplored rigidity of our American written constitutions has made us fear we would not solve short of revolution or of civil war."

That this new and novel doctrine will yet play

[1] See *The American Review of Reviews*, vol. xlv., p. 567 (issue for May, 1912).

an important part in the political and judicial history of our country can hardly be doubted. It may not be adopted in the form that it has taken in the hands of its author and chief defender, but it is easy to see that it must offer suggestions of great practical importance to the political reformers of the immediate future, and it is not an impossibility that it may be tried out in its present form in some progressive state of the American Union before another national campaign has spent its force and accomplished its victories or suffered its defeats.

CHAPTER XII

CONCLUSION

IT is an interesting fact that most of the fundamental questions which have produced a difference of opinion between the political parties have found solution in the Federal courts. Practically the only important question that was not submitted to the Supreme Court was that of internal improvements, and the issue on which it was contested found solution in similar questions before the courts. More and more are the American people looking to the Federal courts as the final arbiter of their political issues. Their willingness to abide their decree is the best evidence of the supreme confidence that is imposed in these tribunals. It is fortunate that this confidence exists, for it insures the country against riots and civil strife resulting from heated debate and party antagonisms.

The courts have, by virtue of judicial power over statutes, become a great power in controlling and extending our nationality. The courts have been able to settle the metes and bounds of practically every issue considered, with the exception of that of slavery. Bryce says, that "it is hardly an exaggeration to say that the American Constitution as it now stands, with the mass of fringing decisions which explain it, is a far more complete and finished instrument than it was when it came fire-new from the hands of the Convention. It is not merely their work but the work of the judges, and most of all the work of one man, the great Chief Justice Marshall."

It is also interesting to consider the important function played by the political parties of this country. We have come almost to consider them a part of the administrative forces of our government. The extreme idea of coördinating the legislative and executive departments of our national Government has made the harmony between the making and the execution of the law very slight. It is the function of the political party to produce a closer harmony between these two branches of our Government. Goodnow says:[1]

"Owing to the slight control which the Legislature has over the executive, the necessary harmony between the making and the execution of the law has to be secured outside of the governmental system. The attempt is made to secure it through the political party which, as a result of political necessity, has obtained during our century or more of political development great strength."

Further on in the same chapter this author says:

"The independence of the executive, which appears so great upon a consideration of the con-

[1] *Principles of the Administrative Law of the United States*, p. 48.

stitution, disappears when we consider his position from the point of view of actual political practice. The needs of practical political life take from the executive his independence, and render him responsible to an extra-governmental organization. This is the administrative side. On the political side the parties are constantly formulating issues, creating public sentiment, and using the political machinery to carry these issues into laws."

The law is the finished product from the political factory. If it is then able to stand the test of the courts, it is then made a part of our legal equipment. "In America," says Bryce, "the government goes for less than in Europe, the parties count for more. The great moving forces are the parties." When we consider both the administrative and political functions of the parties in this country, the truth of this statement is most evident.

There has been a striking parallel between the functions of the English and American parties. According to Macaulay,[1] modern parties in England had their origin in 1641, when the English Parliament was considering the Great Remonstrance to Charles I. They were first called "Roundheads" and "Cavaliers" and subsequently "Whigs" and "Tories." In generalizing on the basis of the difference between them, Macaulay says:

"Everywhere there is a class of men who cling

[1] *History of England*, vol. i., chapter i.

with fondness to whatever is ancient, and who, even when convinced by overpowering reasons that innovations would be beneficial, consent to it with many misgivings and forebodings. We find also everywhere another class of men, sanguine in hope, bold in speculation, always pressing forward, quick to discern the imperfections of whatever exists, disposed to think lightly of the risks of change, and disposed to give every change credit for being an improvement."

This contrast is a rather fair characterization of the Democrats on the one hand, and the Whigs and the Republicans on the other. The Democrats have clung with fondness to the time-honored customs, and have looked on most changes with "misgivings and forebodings." The Whigs and their successors have been "disposed to think lightly of change, and they have been disposed to give every change credit for being an improvement." This has made the Whig and Republican parties the great constructive agencies, while it has been no less the important mission of the Democratic party to compel a sufficient degree of conservatism to prevent innovations which might prove harmful.

The doctrine of strict construction has been the Democratic weapon, with which it has fought radicalism; and while the principle of loose construction has long been recognized, as has been shown, still the constant appeal of the Democratic party to strict construction, has been effective in keeping the law within speaking distance of the

Constitution. The doctrine of strict construction was the principal tenet of the early Republicans or, as they were sometimes called, Democratic-Republicans. The Federalists of Washington's administration were loose constructionists. We must not fall into the error of supposing that the Republicans were simply the old Anti-Federalists under a new name; or that the Federalists of Washington's administration were the same as the Federalists of an earlier date. The fact is, that with the actual beginning of our national existence, a general reorganization of our political parties took place. For instance, Madison, and other strong Federalists of 1791, in Washington's administration became Republicans with Jefferson, and the advocates of strict construction. Many former Federalists aligned themselves with the Republicans in opposing the financial plans of Hamilton. From that time on the Democratic party has adhered to strict construction as a cardinal principle.

Woodburn[1] finds the continuing basis of division of the parties in constitutional construction and the degree of centralization.

"In these two differences,—in constitutional construction and in the differing attitudes of the two parties toward liberty and government,— writers have found the 'continuing basis of division' between the two great historic parties in America. One party, known by its several names,

[1] *Political Parties and Party Problems in the United States*, p. 20.

246 Interpretation of Political Theory

Federalist, Whig, Republican, has favored broad
construction, the growth of national power, increasing functions of government, the larger exercise of force and authority in restraint of social
disorders. The other party, under its various
names Anti-Federalist, Democratic-Republican,
has held to strict construction, the rights of the
state to the largest degree of individual and social
liberty, without annoyance from government. The
one of these parties has been called the party of
political measures, the other the party of political
principles. The one, the Federalist-Whig-Republi-
can, were the advocates of governmental schemes
and projects, the financial plans of Hamilton,
the excise, the Alien and Sedition Acts, the protective policy, internal improvements, Congressional
restraint of slavery, energetic measures in prosecu-
tion of the Civil War and Congressional Reconstruction. The other party, from its principles
of attachment to individual liberty and constitutional restraint on government, has usually
opposed these measures for the purpose of preventing government from attempting too many things
on behalf of the people and for the purpose of
preventing objectionable measures urged on behalf
of special and powerful interests."

The continuing basis of division is described by
Bryce[1] as follows:

"Two permanent oppositions may be discerned
running through the history of the parties, sometimes openly recognized, sometimes concealed by
the urgency of a transitory question. One of
these is the opposition between a centralized or

[1] *American Commonwealth* (Abridged Edition), p. 464.

unitary and a federalized government. State au-
tonomy was the watchword of the Democratic
party. The wish to increase the range and force
of the national Government, seldom distinctly
avowed, was generally in fact represented by the
Federalists of the first period, the Whigs of the
second, the Republicans of the third. The other
opposition, though it goes deeper and is more
pervasive, has been less clearly marked in America, and less consciously admitted by the Americans themselves. It is the opposition between the
tendency which makes some men prize the freedom of the individual as the first of social goods,
and that which disposes others to insist on check-
ing and regulating his impulses. The opposition
of these two tendencies—love of liberty and love
of order—is permanent and necessary, because it
springs from differences in intellect and feelings of
men which appear in all countries and at all
epochs."

The party history of this country may be
roughly divided into four periods. 1. *The first
period from 1787 to 1789.* The short period of the
Federalists and the Anti-Federalists in which the
Constitution itself was really the platform of one
of the parties. "On the one side was arrayed
those who believed in a strong central government; against them were pitted those who believed
that their well tried local and state governments
were in danger."[1]

2. *The second period from 1789 to 1832.* This
period was one of origins. It saw the beginning

[1] See Macy's *Political Parties in the United States*, p. 46.

of the tariff issue, the conflict over the national bank, and internal improvements. It witnessed the destruction of the Federalist party and the rise of personal politics with the personality of Clay and Adams in conflict with the intense personality of Jackson.

3. *The third period from 1832 to 1856.* This period is coexistent with the life history of the Whigs. This party had its origin in opposition to the Jacksonian Democrats, who were the strict adherents to the principles of Jefferson. The issues of the periods were the Second United States Bank, the Tariff, Internal Improvements, the sub-treasury during the latter part of the period, and the Executive Veto. The fundamental issues were inherited from the preceding period.

4. *The fourth period from 1856 to 1860.* The period that brought the abolition and free soil elements together into the newly formed Republican party on the single issue of slavery.

5. *The fifth period from 1860 to 1876.* The period of war measures and reconstruction. The period was one in which the problems of finance were the most perplexing. The solution was found in a continuation of the protective tariff, income tax, and legal tender. The period was marked by a large extension of nationality, as has been shown.

6. *The sixth period from 1876 to the present time.* The issues between the two dominant parties have not been so clearly drawn during this period.

The public questions have related to the tariff, reform in the governmental service, the monetary question, imperialism, and the control of the trusts. The only important constitutional issues are those relating to the trusts and imperialism. The creation of the Interstate Commerce Commission by Congress and the Anti-Trust Act, known as the Sherman Act, and the recognition of these acts as constitutional by the Supreme Court has eliminated the trust as an issue. The tariff laws with reference to our insular possessions and the attitude of the courts with reference to these laws have almost eliminated this question also from the realm of political controversy. However, there will doubtless be other questions of a fundamental nature to arise with reference to the Philippines, and perhaps in connection with Porto Rico, which will produce intense party differences for many years to come.

An examination of the scope and nature of the problems which have been considered, forces the conclusion that most of the fundamental problems and questions relating to our national existence and fundamental law have found final solution.

"The Constitution of the United States, in its principles and in its main features, is no longer the subject of controversy, of debate, or of doubt.

"The line of sovereignty in the states and the nature, extent, and limits of the sovereignty of the national Government have been distinctly marked; and thus the gravest questions that have arisen under the Constitution—questions that disturbed the harmony and threatened the existence of the Union—have passed from the field of debate into the realm of settled law."[1]

[1] Preface to Boutwell's *The Constitution of the United States at the end of the First Century.*

APPENDICES

PARTY PRINCIPLES ON NATIONAL ISSUES[1]

A

JUDICIAL POWER OVER LEGISLATIVE ENACTMENTS

Ultimate Jurisdiction of Supreme Court Recognized.

"Resolved, That the Supreme Court of the United States is the only tribunal recognized by the Constitution for deciding in the last resort all questions arising under the Constitution and laws of the United States, and that upon the preservation of the authority and jurisdiction of that court inviolate depends the existence of the nation." Fourth resolution of the National Republican Convention of 1832.[2]

"Resolved, That the Democratic party will abide by the decisions of the Supreme Court of the United States on the questions of constitutional law." Second resolution of the Democratic Platform of 1860.

[1] The positive views have been placed on the left and the negative views on the right, without regard to the party holding them. It is hoped in this way to give emphasis to the great assertive principles of all parties.

[2] Previous to 1832 no national conventions were held and no party platforms issued.

251

B

THEORY OF CONSTITUTIONAL CONSTRUCTION

Strict Construction Advocated.

"Resolved, That the Federal government is one of *limited powers*, derived solely from the Constitution, and the grants of power shown therein ought to be *strictly construed* by all the departments and agents of the government, and that it is inexpedient and dangerous to exercise doubtful constitutional powers." First resolution of the Democratic Platform of 1840, and reaffirmed in exactly the same language in the Democratic Platforms of 1844, 1848, and 1852.

"The Government of the United States is of a limited character, and is *confined to the exercise of powers expressly granted by the Constitution*, and such as may be necessary and proper for carrying the granted powers into full execution, and that powers not granted or necessarily implied are reserved to the states respectively and to the people." First declaration of the Whig Platform of 1852.

"Resolved, That all governmental powers, whether state or federal, are trust powers coming from the people of each state, and that they are *limited to the written letter of the Constitution* and the laws passed in the pursuance of it; which powers must be exercised in the utmost good faith, the Constitution itself stating in what manner they may be altered and amended." Second resolution of the Democratic Platform of 1872.

C

THEORY OF THE FEDERAL UNION

Union a Nation, not a League.

'The federal and state governments are parts of one system, alike necessary for the common prosperity, peace, and security, and ought to be regarded alike with a cordial, habitual, and immovable attachment. Respect for the authority of each, and acquiescence in the just constitutional measures of each, are duties required by the plainest considerations of national, state, and individual welfare." Whig Platform of 1852.

"The United States of America *is a nation, not a league.* By the combined workings of the national and state governments, under their respective constitutions, the rights of every citizen are secured, at home and abroad, and the common welfare promoted." Section 1 of the Republican Platform of 1876.

"The Constitution of the United States is a supreme law, and not a mere contract. Out of confederated states it made a sovereign nation. Some powers are denied to the nation, while others are denied to the states; but the boundary

Opposition to Centralization.

"Resolved, That the original basis of our whole political structure is consent in every part thereof.[1] The people of each state voluntarily created their state, and the states voluntarily formed the Union; and each state provided by its written constitution for everything a state could do for the protection of life, liberty, and property within it; and each state, jointly with the others, provided a federal union for foreign and interstate relations." First resolution of the (Straight-Out) Democratic Platform of 1872.

"Opposition to centralization and to that dangerous spirit of encroachment which tends to consolidate the powers of all the departments in one, and thus to create, whatever be the form of government, a real despotism." Section 2 of the Democratic Platform of 1880.

"We believe . . . a return to the·fundamental principles of a free popular government, based on home rule and individual liberty, was never more urgent than now, when the

[1] See also the Virginia and Kentucky Resolutions (1798 and 1799) prepared by Madison and Jefferson, the leaders of the Republican party. These resolutions have been called the first party platform in America.

between the powers delegated and those reserved is to be determined by the national and not by the state tribunal." Section 2 of the Republican Platform of 1880.

"The people of the United States, in their organized capacity, constitute a nation, and not an American federacy of states. The national government is supreme within the sphere of its national duties; but the states have reserved rights which should be faithfully maintained. Each should be guarded with jealous care, so that the harmony of our system of government may be preserved and the Union kept inviolate." Republican Platform of 1884.

tendency to centralize all power at the federal capital has become a menace to the reserved rights of the states that strikes at the roots of our government, under the Constitution as framed by the fathers of the republic." Section 1 of the Democratic Platform of 1892.

D

IMPERIALISM v. EXPANSION

Opposition to Imperialism.

"We hold that the Constitution follows the flag, and denounce the doctrine that an executive or Congress deriving their existence and their powers from the Constitution can exercise lawful authority beyond it or in violation of it.

"We assert that no nation can long endure half republic and half empire, and we warn the American people that imperialism abroad will lead quickly and inevitably to despotism at home.

"We are not opposed to territorial expansion when it takes in desirable territory which can be erected into states in the Union, and whose

Control of Non-Contiguous Territory Favored.

"Our foreign policy should be at all times firm, vigorous, and dignified, and all our interests in the Western Hemisphere carefully watched and guarded. The Hawaiian Islands should be controlled by the United States, and no foreign power should be permitted to interfere with them." Republican Platform of 1896.

"We approve the annexation of the Hawaiian Islands to the United States." Republican Platform of 1900.

"In accepting, by the Treaty of Paris, the just responsibility people are willing and fit to become American citizens. We favor expansion by every peaceful and legitimate means. But we are unalterably opposed to seizing or purchasing distant lands to be governed outside the Constitution, and whose people can never become citizens." The "paramount issue" in the Democratic Platform of 1900.

"We favor the preservation, so far as we can, of an open door for the world's commerce in the Orient, without an unnecessary entanglement in Oriental and European affairs, and without arbitrary, unlimited, irresponsible, and absolute government anywhere within our jurisdiction. We oppose, as fervently as did George Washington himself, an indefinite, irresponsible, discretionary, and vague absolutism and a policy of Colonial exploitation, no matter where or by whom invoked or exercised. We believe, with Thomas Jefferson and John Adams, that no government has a right to make one set of laws for those 'at home' and another and a different set of laws, absolute in their character, for those 'in the colonies.' All men under the American flag are entitled to the protection of the institutions whose emblem the flag is. If they are inherently unfit for those institutions, then they are inherently unfit to be members of the American body politic. Wherever there may exist a people incapable of being governed under American laws, in consonance with the Ameri-

of our victories in the Spanish war, the President and the Senate won the undoubted approval of the American people. No other course was possible than to destroy Spain's sovereignty throughout the West Indies and in the Philippine Islands. That course created our responsibility before the world and with the unorganized population whom our intervention had freed from Spain, to provide for the maintenance of law and order, and for the establishment of good government, and for the performance of international obligations.

"Our authority could not be less than our responsibility, and wherever sovereign rights were extended it became the high duty of the government to maintain its authority, to put down armed insurrection, and to confer the blessings of liberty and civilization upon all the rescued peoples." Republican Platform of 1900.

can Constitution, the territory of that people ought not to be a part of the American domain.

"We insist that we ought to do for the Filipinos what we have done already for the Cubans, and it is our duty to make that promise now, and upon suitable guarantees of protection to citizens of our own and other countries resident there at the time of our withdrawal, set the Philippine people upon their feet, free and independent to work out their own destiny." Democratic Platform of 1904.

E

THE THEORY OF INTERNAL IMPROVEMENT

Congressional Power Upheld.	*Congressional Power Denied.*
"Resolved, That a uniform system of internal improvements, sustained and supported by the general government, is calculated to secure, in the highest degree, the harmony, the strength, and the permanency of the republic." Third resolution in the Platform of the National Republican party of 1832.	"Resolved, That the Constitution does not confer upon the general government the power to commence and carry on a general system of internal improvements." Democratic Platform of 1840, and reaffirmed in each succeeding Platform of this party until 1856.
"Resolved, That river and harbor improvements, when demanded by the safety and convenience of commerce with foreign nations, or among the several states, are objects of national concern, and that it is the duty of Congress, in the exercise of its constitutional power, to provide therefor." Thirteenth resolution of the Platform of the Free-Soil party of 1848.	

"Resolved, That appropriations by Congress for the improvement of rivers and harbors of a national character, required for the accommodation and security of our existing commerce, are authorized by the Constitution and justified by the obligations of the government to protect the lives and property of its citizens." Republican Platform of 1856.

F

THE THEORY OF A UNITED STATES BANK

Congressional Power Denied.

"Resolved, That Congress has no power to charter a United States Bank; that we believe such an institution one of deadly hostility to the best interests of the country, dangerous to our republican institutions and the liberties of the people, and calculated to place the business of the country within the control of a concentrated money power and above the laws and the will of the people." Resolution number 6 of the Democratic Platform of 1840, and reaffirmed in the Platform of 1844.

To the above was added the following in the Democratic Platform of 1856: "and that the results of Democratic legislation in this and all other financial measures upon which issues have been made between the two political parties of the country have demonstrated to candid and practical men of all parties, their soundness, safety, and utility in all business pursuits."

G

Congressional Power Upheld.

"Resolved, That these principles may be summarized as follows: A well-regulated currency, etc." From Whig Platform of 1844.

"Resolved, . . . that it is the duty of every loyal state to sustain the credit and promote the use of the national currency." Republican [Regular] Platform of 1864.

"A uniform national currency has been provided, repudiation frowned down, the national credit sustained under the most extraordinary burdens, and new bonds negotiated at lower rates." Republican Platform of 1872.

"The right to make and issue money is a sovereign power, to be maintained by the people for their common benefit. The delegation of this right to corporations is a surrender of the central attribute of sovereignty, void of constitutional sanction, and conferring upon a subordinate and irresponsible power an absolute dominion over industry and commerce. All money, whether metallic or paper, should be issued, and its volume controlled, by the government, and not by or through banking corporations; and when so issued, should be a full legal tender for all debts public and private." Greenback Platform of 1880.

Congressional Power Denied.

"We declare unqualified hostility to bank notes and paper money as a circulating medium, because gold and silver is the only safe and constitutional currency." From the Declaration of the Democrats of New York, in 1836, which was generally accepted as a national party declaration.

"One currency for the government and the people, the laborer and the officeholder, the pensioner and the soldier, the producer and the bondholder." Democratic Platform of 1868.

"A speedy return to specie payment is demanded alike by the highest considerations of commercial morality and honest government." Liberal Republican Platform of 1872.

"Reform is necessary to establish a sound currency, restore the public credit, and maintain the national honor." Democratic Platform of 1876.

"We believe in honest money, the gold and silver of the Constitution, and a circulating medium convertible into such money without loss." Democratic Platform of 1884.

"Congress alone has the power to coin and issue money and President Jackson declared that this power could not be delegated to corpora-

"That we hold the late decision of the Supreme Court on the legal tender question to be a full vindication of the theory which our party has always advocated on the right and authority of Congress over the issue of legal-tender notes, and we hereby pledge ourselves to uphold said decision, and to defend the Constitution against alterations or amendments intended to deprive the people of any rights or privileges conferred by that instrument. . . . We demand the substitution of greenbacks for national-bank notes, and the prompt payment of the public debt. We want that money which saved our country in time of war and which has given it prosperity and happiness in peace." Greenback Platform of 1884.

tions or individuals. We therefore denounce the issuance of notes intended to circulate as money by national banks as in derogation of the Constitution, and we demand that all paper which is made a legal tender for public and private debts, or which is receivable for dues to the United States, shall be issued by the government of the United States, and shall be redeemable in coin." Democratic Platform of 1896.

H

THE THEORY OF A PROTECTIVE TARIFF

Protection Favored.

"An adequate protection to American industry is indispensable to the prosperity of the country; and that an abandonment of the policy at this period would be attended with consequences ruinous to the best interests of the nation." Republican Platform of 1832.

"The revenue necessary for current expenditures and the obligations of the public debt must be largely derived from duties upon importations, which, as far as possible, should be adjusted to promote the interests of American labor

Tariff for Revenue Only.

"That justice and sound policy forbid the federal government to foster one branch of industry to the detriment of another, or to cherish the interests of one portion to the injury of another portion of our common country." Democratic Platform of 1840.

"A tariff for revenue to defray the necessary expenses of the government." From the summary of the principles of the Whig Platform of 1844.

"That we favor a judicious tariff *for revenue purposes only,* and advance the prosperity of the whole country." Republican Platform of 1876.

"We therefore demand that the imposition of duties on foreign imports shall be made not for 'revenue only,' but that in raising the requisite revenues for the government such duties shall be so levied as to afford security to our diversified industries and protection to the rights and wages of the laborer, to the end that active and intelligent labor, as well as capital, may have its just rewards, and the laboring man his full share in the national prosperity." Republican Platform of 1884.

"We are uncompromisingly in favor of the American system of protection; we protest against its destruction as proposed by the President and his party. They serve the interests of Europe; we will support the interests of America. We accept the issue and confidently appeal to the people for their judgment. The protective system must be maintained. Its abandonment has always been followed by general disaster to all interests, except those of the usurer and the sheriff. We denounce the Mills Bill as destructive to the general business, the labor, and the farming interests of the country, and we heartily indorse the consistent and patriotic action of the Republican representatives in Congress in opposing its passage." Republican Platform of 1888.

"We reaffirm the American doctrine of protection. We

and that we are unalterably opposed to class legislation which enriches a few at the expense of many, under the plea of protection." Democratic Platform of 1872.

"Congress should modify the tariff so as to admit free such articles of common use as we can neither produce nor grow, and lay duties for revenue mainly upon articles of luxury and upon such articles of manufacture as will, we having the raw material, assist in further developing the resources of the country." Labor Reform party Platform of 1872.

"We denounce the present tariff, levied upon nearly 4000 articles, as a masterpiece of injustice, inequality, and false pretense. It yields a dwindling, not a yearly rising revenue. It has impoverished many industries to subsidize a few. It prohibits imports that might purchase the products of American labor. It has degraded American commerce from the first to an inferior rank on the high seas. It has cut down the sales of American manufactures at home and abroad, and depleted the returns of American agriculture —an industry followed by half of our people. It costs the people five times more than it produces to the treasury, obstructs the processes of production, and wastes the fruits of labor. It prompts fraud, fosters smuggling, enriches dishonest officials, and bankrupts honest merchants. We demand that all custom-house taxation shall be only for call attention to its growth abroad. We maintain that the prosperous condition of our country is largely due to the wise revenue legislation of the last Republican Congress. We believe that all articles which cannot be produced in the United States, except luxuries, should be admitted free of duty, and that on all imports coming into competition with the products of American labor there should be levied duties equal to the difference between w a g e s abroad and at home." Republican Platform of 1892.

"We renew and emphasize our allegiance to the policy of protection as the bulwark of American industrial independence and the foundation of American development and prosperity. This true American policy taxes foreign products and encourages home industry; it puts the burden of revenue on foreign goods; it secures the American market for the American producer; it upholds the American standard of wages for the American workingman; it puts the factory by the side of the farm, and makes the American farmer less dependent on foreign demand and price; it diffuses general thrift, and founds the strength of all on the strength of each. In its reasonable application it is just, fair, and impartial; equally opposed to foreign control and domestic monopoly, to sectional discrimination a n d individual favoritism." Republican Platform of 1896.

"We renew our faith in the

revenue." Democratic Platform of 1876.

"Sufficient revenue to pay all expenses of the federal government economically administered, including pensions, interest and principal of the public debt, can be got under our present system of taxation from the custom-house taxes on fewer imported articles, bearing heaviest on articles of luxury and bearing lightest on articles of necessity." Democratic Platform of 1884.

"Our established domestic industries and enterprises should not and need not be endangered by the reduction and correction of the burdens of taxation. On the contrary, a fair and careful revision of our tax laws, with due allowance for the difference between the wages of American and foreign labor, must promote and encourage every branch of such industries and enterprises, by giving them assurance of an extended market and steady and continuous operations. . . . Upon this question of tariff reform so closely concerning every phase of our national life, and upon every question involved in the problem of good government, the Democratic party submits its principles and professions to the intelligent suffrages of the American people." Democratic Platform of 1888.

"We denounce Republican protection as a fraud—a robbery of the great majority of the American people for the benefit of the few. We declare policy of protection to American labor. In that policy our industries have been established, diversified, and maintained. By protecting the home market, competition has been stimulated and production cheapened. Opportunity to the inventive genius of our people has been secured and wages in every department of labor maintained at high rates —higher now than ever before, and always distinguishing our working people in their better condition of life from those of any competing country." Republican Platform of 1900.

"Protection which guards and develops our industries is a cardinal policy of the Republican party. *The measure of protection should always at least equal the difference in the cost of production at home and abroad.*" Republican Platform of 1904.

it to be a fundamental principle of the Democratic party *that the federal government has no constitutional power to impose and collect tariff duties, except for the purposes of revenue only,* and we demand that the collection of such taxes shall be limited to the necessities of the government when honestly and economically administered." Democratic Platform of 1892.

"Tariff should be levied only as a defense against the foreign governments which levy tariff upon or bar out our products from their markets, revenue being incidental. The residue of means necessary to an economical administration of the government should be raised by levying a burden on what the people possess instead of upon what they consume." National Prohibition Platform of 1892.

"Tariff laws should be amended by putting the products of trusts upon the free list, to prevent monopoly under the plea of protection." Democratic Platform of 1900.

"The Democratic party has been and will continue to be the consistent opponent of that class of tariff legislation by which certain interests have been permitted, through Congressional favor, to draw a heavy tribute from the American people. This monstrous prevention of those equal opportunities which our political institutions were established to secure has caused what may once have been infant industries to become the greatest combinations of capital that the world has ever known. These especial favorites of the government have, through trust methods, been converted into monopolies, thus bringing to an end domestic competition, which was the only alleged check upon the extravagant profits made possible by the protective system.

"We denounce protection as a robbery of the many to enrich the few, and we favor a tariff limited to the needs of the government economically administered, and so levied as not to discriminate against any industry, class, or section, to the end that the burdens of taxation shall be distributed as equally as possible." Democratic Platform of 1904.

I

THE THEORY OF AN INCOME TAX

Income Tax Favored.

"A graduated income-tax is the most equitable system of taxation, placing the burden of government on those who can best afford to pay, instead of laying it on the farmers and producers, and exempting millionaire bondholders and corporations." The Union Labor Platform of 1888.

"We demand a graduated income-tax." National People's Party Platform of 1892.

"We demand . . . a progressive income-tax and tax on inheritances; the smaller incomes to be exempt." Socialist-Labor Platform of 1892.

"We demand a graduated income-tax, to the end that aggregate wealth shall bear its just proportion of taxation, and we denounce the recent decision of the Supreme Court relative to the income-tax law as a misinterpretation of the Constitution and an invasion of the rightful powers of Congress over the subject of taxation." People's party Platform of 1896.

"We demand a levy and collection of a graduated tax on incomes and inheritances, and a constitutional amendment to secure same, if necessary." People's party Platform of 1900. Also found in the Silver Republican Platform of 1900.

"We congratulate the country upon the triumph of an important reform demanded in the last national platform— namely, the amendment of the federal constitution authorizing an income tax." Democratic Platform of 1912.

J

THE THEORY OF DIRECT LEGISLATION

Initiative, Referendum, and Recall Advocated.

"We commend to the thoughtful consideration of the people and the reform press, the legislative system known as the initiative and referendum." National People's party Platform of 1892.

"The people have the right to propose laws and to vote upon all measures of impor-

tance, according to the referendum   principle." Social-
Labor Platform of 1892.

"We favor a system of
direct legislation through the
initiative and referendum,
under proper constitutional
safeguards." People's party
Platform of 1896.

"The initiative and referendum, and proportional representation, should be adopted."
National party Convention of
1896.

"We demand the initiative
and referendum, and the imperative mandate for such
changes of existing fundamental and statute law as will enable the people in their sovereign capacity to propose and
compel the enactment of such
laws as they desire, to reject
such as they deem injurious to
their interests, and to recall
unfaithful public servants."
People's party Platform of
1900.

K

THEORY OF THE RECALL OF JUDICIAL DECISIONS

Recall of Decisions Advocated.

"The Progressive Party demands such restriction of the
power of the courts as should
leave to the people the ultimate authority to determine
fundamental questions of social
welfare and public policy. To
secure this end it pledges itself
to provide:
" 1. That when an act,
passed under the police power

of the State, is held unconstitutional under the State Constitution by the courts, the
people, after an ample interval
for deliberation, shall have an
opportunity to vote on the
question whether they desire
the act to become a law, notwithstanding such decision.

"2.   That every decision of
the highest appellate court of
a State declaring an act of the
Legislature unconstitutional on
the ground of its violation of
the federal constitution shall
be subject to the same review
by the Supreme Court of the
United States as is now accorded to decisions sustaining
such legislation." Progressive
(Republican) Platform of 1912.

INDEX OF CASES

A

PAGE

GENERAL INDEX

A

Act, Legal Tender, 153
Adams, J. Q., on internal improvements, 116
Amendment, Sixteenth, 197
American doctrine of judicial supremacy, 27
Andrews, E. Benjamin, on legal-tender cases, 163
Anti-Federalist, origin of, 47

B

Bagehot on legislative supremacy in England, 24
Bailey, Senator, on constitutionality of income tax, 194
Bascom's criticism of the income tax decision, 193
Beveridge on imperialism, 92
Binney, Horace, on function of Supreme Court, 3
Blackstone on legislative supremacy in England, 24
Bourne, Senator, on direct legislation, 223
Broom, Herbert, on law as an inexact science, 4
Bryce, on early recognition of judicial supremacy, 32; political issues and court decrees, 46; on necessity of loose construction, 63; influence on direct legislation, 207; on basis of party cleavage, 246
Bunderstadt, 47

C

Calhoun on internal improvements, 111
Carson on party conviction and court decrees, 4
Chase, appointed Chief Justice 13; opinion on State banking acts, 140; on legal-tender acts, 153
Choate, Rufus, on the case of Marbury *v*. Martin, 43
Civil Law, doctrine of judicial supremacy under, 22
Clay, opposition to Taney, 9; on internal improvements, 107; attitude toward bank, 125; sponsor of the protective theory, 167; nominated for presidency, 171
Coke, Lord, natural justice theory and court supremacy, 25
Convention, free trade, 170
Court, General, of Massachusetts, 204
Coxe, Brinton, on judicial supremacy in the civil law, 21; on judicial supremacy in English law, 25
Crises, nullification pamphlet, 170
Cullom Act, 80

D

De Tocqueville on peril of imperialistic government, 103
Dicey on legislative supremacy, 26